The
Birth of
The Church

THE
BIRTH OF
THE CHURCH

G. Campbell Morgan

EDITED BY JILL MORGAN

Fleming H. Revell Company
Old Tappan, New Jersey

Foreword

Most of Dr. Morgan's published works were, to quote from the foreword in his volume on *The Gospel According to Mark,* "stenographically reported, and . . . now issued . . . with no revision beyond the simplest elimination of repetitions and asides, which, while giving force to the extempore utterance, would render the reading tiresome."

The quotation could also apply to this hitherto unpublished work with slight but important differences. This stenographically reported manuscript was never edited or given a title by the author himself, the probable reason being lack of time or opportunity, inasmuch as the lectures were delivered during that period of his itinerant ministry in the United States when he was constantly on the move from one city to another.

Moreover, these "utterances" are not sermons in the accepted sense of the word, in that they are lectures given during a two-week period, Monday through Friday, to a group who came with Bibles and notebooks for the study of the Word. In the course of these studies Dr. Morgan says: "I am not preaching. We are just taking our way through the passage, working together as students."

In reading the unedited manuscript for the first time, one fact emerged most strongly—the informal, conversational method of delivery, as one would talk to and with a group of friends on a subject of mutual interest. Though the lectures were given in other places, this series was reported in Tacoma, Washington, during a Lenten season. It is evident that many ministers attended, and a number of young people also. While eliminating some repetition, which is always necessary for the orientation of those who may have missed a previous lecture, we have tried to retain the charm and intimacy of the tone and method of a teacher who is entirely *en rapport* with his students.

These lectures exemplify Dr. Morgan at his "teaching best." Indirectly, they reveal the careful and painstaking preparation which issues in a seemingly effortless result. A special note is in order here—the fact that a good teacher, no matter how knowledgeable and dedicated, is always open-minded to another point of view. At the time the lectures were delivered, Dr. Morgan believed that the "one place" of Acts 2:1, where those were assembled when they received the gift of the Holy Spirit, was the same as the "upper room" of Acts 1:13, as he intimates in the first lecture. At a later date he changed his views regarding the locale after reading a booklet entitled *Where Did the Holy Spirit Descend at Pentecost?*, written by Mr. Philip Mauro, a friend whose Biblical scholarship he respected. Mr. Mauro's findings led him to believe that a room in the Temple was the more likely site, inasmuch as there was no break in God's onward march across the centuries. Dr. Morgan felt that Mr. Mauro was substantiated in his belief that the new movement began in the Temple and from thence moved out to the uttermost part of the earth, thus maintaining perfect continuity.

Dr. Morgan preferred the American Standard Version as a study text. However, the Bible in its entirety was so familiar to him that he quoted many times from memory, sometimes using the American Standard Version, sometimes the King James Version, sometimes the marginal references in either, and sometimes, for the sake of clarity, using a free translation of his own. In commenting on this we can do no better than quote the comment he makes himself in chapter 7:

". . . Peter did not quote the exact words of the Psalm (16), but he did not alter the sense by a single touch. The sense is the same, but not the words . . . no New Testament speaker, even Jesus Himself or others, quoted exactly from the Hebrew Scriptures. They changed the wording but they never changed the sense."

We make no apology for the title, *The Birth of the Church,* for that is the way Dr. Morgan himself refers to that most auspicious date in history—the Pentecost of the second chapter of the Book of Acts.

J. M.

The
Birth of
The Church

CHAPTER • 1

ACTS 2:1-4

In this second chapter of the Acts we have the history of the very beginning of the Christian Church, and of the first things of its life, and light, and love. We are away back in the heights of the mountains where the springs came up, that have broadened into the great river of the centuries, and I am inclined to indulge for a moment in parabolic reference. Years ago in England there was a man who was a colporteur of the British and Foreign Bible Society, an agent, who became quite famous in a certain way as a literary man. I am referring to George Borrow. Some of you may have read that very wonderful book of his, *The Bible in Spain.* He wrote another book which he called *Wild Wales.* I refer to it now only because he tells how, when he climbed Plynlimmon mountain his guide took him to the place where the springs bubble up that are the sources of three rivers, the Severn, the Wye, and the Rheidol. He says that when he looked at those little springs bubbling up, that presently were to become those three rivers, he said to his guide this strange thing: "Now," he said, "bring me some of that water to drink, so that in days to come, when I harangue about my visit here, I may do it with authority, having drunk of the waters at the fountainhead." I pray that as we study this wonderful chapter we may not only watch the place where the rivers rise, but drink of the waters ourselves, and know something of its enrichment to our spiritual life.

Today I am going to read the first four verses. I am reading from the American Standard Version. If you are reading from the Authorized Version I raise no objection. I think it is good to say that now, because I shall make reference constantly to the American Standard Version. The King James Version which we call the Authorized abides at the center of our history, the center of our life. So far as its English is concerned it is the most wonderful book that was ever given to the English-speaking race. A great authority has adequately and accurately said that the Authorized Version of the Bible is "a well of English undefiled," and so it surely is, and I am making no objection to anyone's reading it. But I do say to the student of the Bible in English—I am not referring, of course, to those who study their Hebrew Bible or their Greek New Testament —that when you want not only to read the diction but to study as well, you must use the American Standard Version. About that there can be no question.

You will notice some small alterations in this particular passage:

And when the day of Pentecost was now come, they were all together in one place. And suddenly there came from heaven a sound as of the rushing of a mighty wind, and it filled all the house where they were sitting. And there appeared unto them tongues parting asunder, like as of fire; and it sat upon each one of them. And they were all filled with the Holy Spirit, and began to speak with other tongues, as the Spirit gave them utterance.

In those four verses we have a complete story. The moment we are beyond them we are moving into the realm of a second story. When we come to verse 5 we shall see the results produced by that which happened according to the record of these four verses. So today we confine ourselves to these verses; tomorrow we fasten our attention upon one sentence only, but today we are occupied with all the things that surround it. Tomorrow we shall deal with the central sentence—I do not mean as to its place in the paragraph, I mean as to its importance; the great thing of which all the other things were merely signs and evidences—the sentence that declares that they were all filled with the Holy Spirit. That is the central thing that happened. All others are suburban, they are round about it, interesting and valuable, but *that* is the central fact.

Now this paragraph is of value to us because it gives the historic account of the first day of the Christian Church. It is the account of the day upon which that Church was born. A comparison of the Gospel narratives with the Book of the Acts reveals the fact that in all our Lord's earthly ministry He was fulfilling a Messianic mission; and that does not mean that it was merely Jewish or Hebrew, for in the purpose and counsel of God the Messianic mission was not for Israel only, but for all the world. Israel had unquestionably broken down in its understanding of that, and had come to think of itself as a people that God had elected in order that He might have some one nation to lavish His love upon, while He abandoned all the other nations. That was the heresy on which the nation foundered, and lost its place for awhile in the economy of God. Yet there can be no misunderstanding, no mistaking of the fact that our Lord fulfilled His Messianic mission, gathered about Him individual disciples, and, at last, when all His mighty work was over, charged them to tarry until they were endued with power from on high, and that that enduement would come when He would send forth the promise of the Father.

Now in these four verses we have the historic account of the fulfillment of that promise, and on that day the Church was born. So we come back into the mountains where

13

the springs are coming up, and we do well to tarry here, for on that day, for the whole world, a new era began.

If I may interpret the Divine dealing with humanity as it is revealed to us in these holy writings that we call the Bible, I shall do so by saying that in the lifetime of our Lord—that brief space of about three and thirty years, and specifically in that briefer last period of about three and a half years—the Father had at last been revealed through the Incarnate Son. That is what you have, focused in the life of our Lord, the revelation of God through His Son. And infinitely more; not merely revelation, but also all the marvelous carrying out in the historic Being of the Divine and redeeming purpose.

No one perfectly understood the revelation, not one. Not one of the inner circle of His disciples had apprehended the meaning of the things upon which their eyes were looking.

You remember, in the upper room as John records, the last conversation of Jesus with His disciples. He spoke with Philip, the quiet man, the unimpressive man. . . . You say, "Why do you call Philip that?" Well, neither Matthew, Mark, nor Luke make any reference to him beyond naming him in the list of the apostles. They simply named him as one of the twelve. It was John only, whose eyes were always lovelit eyes, who mentioned him on two occasions. But Philip was one of those great souls that every now and then pour out some elemental, human desire; and in the upper room he said, "Show us the Father, and it sufficeth us." No other sentence expressing more of desire and human need at its highest and deepest, ever passed human lips than this: "Show us the Father and it sufficeth us." You remember the answer of Jesus. He said, "Have I been so long time with you, and dost thou not know Me, Philip? He that hath seen Me hath seen the Father." I say, no one had understood Him. Nevertheless the revelation had been given, and they came to understand, *after* the Spirit came as the Interpreter.

14

You remember also in that great passage, in which Paul, when writing to Timothy, gives the most wonderful and poetic mold of truth that is in all your Bible, when he says the Church is "the pillar and ground of the truth," [1] and then breaks out into the great exclamation, "without controversy, great is the mystery of godliness." You remember what follows: "He Who was manifested in the flesh. . . ." Now that covers the whole story of the Incarnation—that one line; and the next sentence: "Justified—or vindicated—in the Spirit"—and the word Spirit, I dogmatically affirm, refers to the Holy Spirit, and should have a capital S. Christ was vindicated, interpreted, justified to the human soul, not in the days of His flesh, but when the Spirit came. But the revelation had been complete. And so, looking back over that brief age in the world's history, the age that we measure by thirty-three years —for the ages of God are not identical in length—with all the light focused on the last three and a half, I repeat, in *that* age, to humanity in the world, God the Father had revealed Himself through the Incarnate Son.

Now, with the coming of the Spirit in this new way, the Son Who revealed the Father is to be interpreted by the Holy Spirit, and no man finds God save through the interpretation of the Spirit. "No man can say, Jesus is Lord, but in the Holy Spirit." [2] That is what we come to in this chapter—the beginning of that movement. There and then the Christian Church was born; the very Body of Christ, the mystical Body, the multiplication of the One into twelve, the five hundred, the three thousand, the five thousand—I am only taking the figures of my New Testament—and then presently the great sacramental host that through more than nineteen hundred years has believed on Him, and has received this very gift of the Holy Spirit. There is the great movement. I repeat, we are back at the very beginning of it in this chapter. Because the Father had been revealed, and in that revelation had wrought

15

out into visibility all His own mighty work on behalf of humanity, the Spirit came to be the Interpreter of the Christ. Now the offer of the eternal grace is to be made, and through the process the preparation for the ultimate glory is to go forth, and that is going forward yet, beloved.

As we deal with the broad outline of these few verses, these are the things we are going to notice: first, the time referred to, "when the day of Pentecost was now come"; secondly, the persons referred to, *"they* were all together"; thirdly, the place, "in one place"; then the symbols, a sound and a sight, a sound "as of . . . a . . . wind," a sight "as of fire"; then the supreme fact, "they were all filled with the Holy Spirit"; and finally the expression of the thing that had happened, they were speaking "with other tongues, as the Spirit gave them utterance."

First, as to the time: "When the day of Pentecost was now come." That is the Revised Version. "And when the day of Pentecost was fully come." So reads the Authorized. Let me at once say to you that another translation carries over this idea —and you will have to be prepared for hearing me say these things. You can correct or verify them by your own study. But if you have got your Revised Version you will find a note in the margin, and it says there, "Gr. 'was being fulfilled.'" Do you get that? Now let me read that again, "And when the day of Pentecost was being fulfilled." Your margin tells you that that is the blunt translation of the Greek, without any attempt to interpret.

Now someone says, "Well, that means the same thing as the other two." Well, does it? Let us stop and think. I maintain that there is really no difference in the intention of the Authorized and the Revised at that point, except that the Revised is not quite as stately as the Authorized. I admit it. "When the day of Pentecost was fully come." "When the day of Pentecost was now come." That means that you have a reference to a date, and that this thing happened on the day of Pentecost, the Hebrew feast. So it does. But now use the margin translation: "When the day of Pentecost was being fulfilled." That means infinitely more than that you have a date. It means that there is a spiritual significance, and that something happened on a date that fulfilled whatever that date had meant in the past. Well, now, that drives the student back to the Old Testament. I am only taking you over familiar ground.

What was the day of Pentecost? If I said that to someone suddenly, on the street or any place, or if I asked you, you would probably say immediately, "The day on which the Spirit fell." It has become that in the Christian Church. But when Luke wrote that, writing from the standpoint of the events he was to record, what did *he* mean by the day of Pentecost? He was referring to a Hebrew feast, he was referring to a Jewish festival, and he distinctly says that this thing happened at that time. Mind, it is a date. I am not quarreling with that, but he says this thing happened on the day of the feast of Pentecost; but he does not say merely that it happened on the day of the feast of Pentecost—he says that the day of Pentecost *was being fulfilled*. The thing that happened that day fulfilled the meaning of the Pentecostal feast.

Very well then, just for a moment put this little paragraph in your Acts beside God's calendar as you find it in the Old Testament; I mean the calendar of all His government of the people, by which He divided the year for the Hebrew nation. He changed a month and made it the first month.[3] You remember that their dating had been otherwise until the point when He gave a national constitution and consciousness to these people.

Hold on a minute. I think I am bound to turn aside here. Of course you will drop out now if you have reconstructed all the Old Testament history. Those who have reconstructed this

17

history, and tell me that all I get in the first five books is post-exilic, and that it is a fraud foisted upon men—well, they will not follow me now. I am taking the history of the Bible as it stands, and as it has never yet been disproven. Very well. God gave to this nation, according to the account, a new calendar, and the month Abib became the first of months. And he interpenetrated the passing of the months with great religious feasts, full of suggestiveness. The first was the feast of Passover. The next, in close association with the feast of Passover, was the feast of unleavened bread. The next in order was the feast of firstfruits. The next was the feast of weeks, and that was fifty days from the feast of firstfruits. The next in order was the feast of trumpets. The next was the day of Atonement; and the last was the feast of tabernacles. The passing of time was marked by the recurrence of the feasts, and the significance of the feasts shed light upon all the days of the Hebrew people. All this is very elementary, I know, but let us look at it for a moment.

The feast of Passover was observed in the first month. What did the Hebrews celebrate? The exodus, the means by which these people came from slavery to be a people unto God. The unleavened bread, closely following Passover, was the feast of communion together of the people separated from slavery to God. Still in the first month, but later on was the feast of firstfruits. (Only, when you read the Bible, remember this: That feast was never observed in the wilderness, never, until they were settled in the land.)

Then came the feast of weeks, fifty days from firstfruits. It was the great bread feast, the feast of harvest in that sense, in the third month. Then, later on in the year, in the seventh month (there was no feast observed between the third and the seventh month) came the feast of trumpets, consummating the gathering of the people together once again—the great feast of trumpets, the realization of the national ideal celebrated, with everything lying behind it. Then came the day of Atonement, and in your thinking never confuse that with the Passover. The day of Atonement was a great day of the annual readjustment of all things in the national life. Then came the last, the great feast, still in the seventh month, the feast of tabernacles, the feast of the settled order. These are the feasts of the Lord, and the Hebrew people observed them every year.

To those who understood, they were all spiritual messages. Every Passover they were reminded of the exodus that made them a people, of their ransom, of their redemption. On each feast of unleavened bread they were reminded of their separation from Egypt and from the nations, and they commemorated the communion of their separation from these things and unto God. Then, when they had entered the land, having crossed the river, they celebrated the feast of firstfruits, their settlement in the land of possession, as the emancipated people. In the feast of weeks they celebrated the fact that all they gathered from the land was given to them by God. It was the great bread feast. In the feast of trumpets they celebrated the consummation of a Divine ideal in their national life. On the day of Atonement there was no celebration. It was not a feast but a fast, a reminder of the consciousness of sin and God's way of dealing with it, the only day in all the year in which one man, and he the high priest, passed into the presence of God. Then came the feast of tabernacles, the settled order, the feast of joy and gladness and rejoicing. When you think of these people, think of the significance of these feasts, set by God.

But those feasts were not only to mark religious truth to the people. They were indicative of the Divine program, God's dealings with men. I wish I could get all our young people to take time to consider those feasts and their relation to all the Divine movements of history.

Now listen to me reverently. The feast of Passover was fulfilled when Jesus was crucified; and the feast of unleavened bread was immediately connected with it in the gathering to Him of a people separated by the mystery of His Cross. And the feast of firstfruits was the feast of resurrection. That is three. Well, you say, that is your imagination. No, I do not often indulge in that with my Bible. I do sometimes, but I will tell you when I am doing that, and I will tell you when I am speculating. I am not speculating now. I am simply taking an interpretation that you will find lying in the very heart of your New Testament. You remember that Paul says, "Christ our passover hath been sacrificed: wherefore let us keep the feast." [4] That is Passover. Directly in connection with it—you will find it in the fifth chapter of I Corinthians—he says, "Wherefore let us keep the feast, not with old leaven, neither with the leaven of malice and wickedness, but with the unleavened bread of sincerity and truth." [5] There is the feast following Passover—the fulfillment. And when you get over to the fifteenth chapter where he is dealing with resurrection, he says, "Christ . . . the firstfruits of them that are asleep." [6]

Now you see how, historically, the suggestiveness of the Hebrew calendar is coming to fulfillment.

Passover was fulfilled at the Cross. When Jesus was on the holy Mount of Transfiguration six months before the Cross, we are told that Moses and Elijah came to Him, and they talked with Him. Now, beloved, let us look at that, shall we? What did they talk about? I am quoting the words you are familiar with. They "spake of his decease which He was about to accomplish at Jerusalem." [7] Decease—what do you mean by decease? Now we have come to use that word "decease" of death, and do you know, that is a very significant and beautiful word. That word was never used of death until Christianity made use of it. It comes from the Latin word "decessus," a going out. They talked of His death, yes, but more than that. They talked of the going out that He should accomplish—the decessus. And the simplest thing to do is to take the Greek word there, of which "decease" is a Latinized equivalent. What is the Greek word? It is "Exodos"—or, to use the English spelling, "exodus." You see what it is. They talked of the exodus that He should accomplish. Christ our Passover is sacrificed for us, and the first great feast of the Hebrew calendar is fulfilled when, in the mystery of His Cross, our Passover was sacrificed and He accomplished the exodus.

Wherefore, says Paul, we keep the feast of unleavened bread. It is the feast of communion of the separated ones with each other, and with the One to Whom they are separated. That began beyond the Cross.

Firstfruits? It is the feast of resurrection—that which brings me into possession of all that God provides for me by the way of the Cross.

What next? Now that is why I insisted upon a literal translation at that point. In the great succession of the Divine movement indicated by that calendar of the Hebrew people —the day of Pentecost, the fifty days' feast beyond firstfruits, the feast of harvest and of bread—Luke says that it was *"being fulfilled."* You see it being fulfilled. You get your narrative in all this chapter.

Just one glance more. What about the other feasts? There are three more; what about them? Have they been fulfilled? I think not. The feast of trumpets is yet to be. When? I have no idea. Neither have you. What beyond it? The day of Atonement. Oh, yes, in one great sense atonement was perfected on Calvary, but its final administration will be beyond the feast of trumpets. And then what? Then the feast of tabernacles. "Behold, the tabernacle of God is with men, and He shall dwell with them. . . ." [8] Do you know where you will find that? It is the ultimate in the Divine economy. Now you take God's calendar, and take *your* history and study it in the light of that, and leave all the rest of them—let them have a rest.

Now, where are we in the second chapter of Acts? "When the day of Pentecost was being fulfilled . . ." marks the dating of the thing that happened. Very well, now step forward. "They were all together. . . ." Who? Well, the narrative is continuous, and in order to answer that I glance back at the first chapter. (Of course it would have been a delightful thing if we had about six months instead of two weeks to go through the first chapter, and then go through the other chapters of Acts.) But you know it, and you have it there.

Chapter 1 is the picture of the disciples before Pentecost, a wonderfully suggestive picture. First you see them gathered round the Lord and asking a question that shows they did not understand even yet, "Lord, dost thou at this time restore the kingdom to Israel?" [9] and you find Him tenderly correcting them. They were not to know times or seasons, but they were to be His witnesses. And then—be patient if you do not agree with the next piece of interpretation—you find them making their first blunder. I know there are some who do not think a blunder was made here. What was it? Electing an apostle instead of waiting. I always hold that the election of Matthias was a mistake; that God had His chosen apostle, and in due season He found him, and Paul came to fill the gap. I do not press that. I am quite sure it is right, but I do not press it. If you think they ought to have elected Matthias, all right. When I get on to the book of Revelation I see the city of God, and in the city of God I am told that on the foundations are the names of the twelve apostles of the Lamb. Which are you going to leave out? Matthias or Paul? I think they had no more right to elect an officer without the power of the Spirit than to try to preach the Gospel; and I think that is true today. Very well, they did it.

Now I go back to see who they were, and it is very beautiful. Verse 13 says: "And when they were come in, they went up into the upper chamber, where they were abiding; both Peter

22

and John. . . ." Some of you young folk, some day get a list of
the apostles in the Gospels, the same ones as are here, and
notice how they are rearranged. It is at least suggestive—they
sort of got mixed up. You see the old associations just changed
round a little. "Peter and John," that is one couple; "and
James and Andrew," that is another; "Philip and Thomas,"
that is another; "Nathanael" (or Bartholomew, the same person) "and Matthew"; James the son of Alphaeus and Simon
the Zealot; and "Judas the son" (which should be the brother)
"of James." There you have eleven of them. "These all with
one accord continued stedfastly in prayer, with the women"—
oh, yes, the women were there—"and Mary the mother of
Jesus, and with His brethren."

That is very wonderful. His brethren after the flesh had
been very much interested in Him; you cannot read the Gospel stories without seeing it. But it does not seem that they
ever committed themselves to Him until the end. It does seem
as though it was the Cross and resurrection that gathered them
in. You will remember that they went to Him once with His
mother to try and persuade Him to come home, and He spoke
those words to the crowd, that those who did the will of His
Father were His mother and brethren. They also tried to get
Him to go up to Jerusalem and to manifest Himself at the
feast of tabernacles, and He said not unkindly, but with a
gentle satire, "My time is not yet come; but your time is
always ready." [10] Now here you find them in the upper room.
There is your group, eleven of them, and the women and
Mary. That is the last reference you find to Mary in your New
Testament. She was there, and his brethren after the flesh.
There they are. Those are the persons.

Now notice that Luke says, "they were all together in one
place." Where? Well, you are bound again to go back to chapter 1. The thirteenth verse says, "And when they were come
in, they went up into the upper chamber." Your familarity

with the East—I do not mean your personal familiarity, though in the case of some of you it *is* personal; but most of you, I suppose, are like me. I have never been in Palestine, but I think I know it. You young people, study the Bible with a map of Palestine before you. I think I know all its hills and valleys and roads. And you and I have acquainted ourselves with the houses of the East. The "upper chamber" referred to a great room which, in those houses, lay over all the other rooms. You know the plan of the houses—the outer court, and then the inner rooms and living room, and the guest chamber; and in the houses of the more wealthy there was this large room running over all the others, under the flat roof. You remember the early Church had its home in the house of Mary, a wealthy woman, living in Jerusalem. This room was suitable for gatherings of people together, often used for that kind of thing; and in such a room these were gathered together. Notice, it was not in the Temple.[11] Jesus had said of that Temple, "Your house is left unto you desolate." [12] This thing did not happen in the Temple. It happened in an ordinary dwelling house. The time was come when no longer in Jerusalem nor on Mount Gerizim would men worship God; and in an ordinary house, in that great upper chamber under the flat roof they were gathered together. So much for the place.

Now to that which happened; not to the essential fact, to which we come tomorrow, save to refer to it, but to the outer symbols. "And suddenly there came from heaven a sound"— not a wind, but a sound—"as of the rushing of a mighty wind." It may have been a wind, but it is the *sound* of the wind that is declared. Now that sound was heard, not only in the upper room but all over the city. Glance down to the sixth verse which is outside our paragraph today, but which we must look at for a moment here, "And when this sound was heard, the multitude came together." There is a change in the rendering here. The Authorized Version reads, "Now when this was noised abroad." Remember, the "noised abroad" is correct, but it does not mean the rumor of it, the talk about it; it means the actual sound. On that day that sound, as of the sweeping of a mighty wind not only filled all that house, but the whole city heard it. It was that sound that brought people rushing together to see what had taken place. Like the sound of a cyclone, yes; but that is not the principal event. It never occurred again. Let us get hold of that right now. It was merely a symbol.

What next? "And there appeared unto them tongues." Beloved, forgive my quiet going over this, but I want you to notice the *little* things. "There appeared unto them tongues parting asunder," or "cloven tongues" as you have it in your Authorized Version. That looks as though every tongue was cloven. Not at all. Now, look—"tongues parting asunder, like as of fire; and *it*" (not they) "sat upon each one of them." One fire, but it divided; the sight of fire, parting, dividing, until on every head in that upper room there was seen by all the rest the tongue like as of fire—not of fire but *like* as of fire. That is the appearing. A sound like a wind, a sight of fire breaking out, disparting. That never happened again. It is quite incidental, nonessential, never to be repeated—and it never was. The sound of the wind, the sight of the fire.

Now I have said twice that this was never repeated. Supposing I turn over for a moment to chapter four, verse 31. "When they had prayed,"—you know when this happened—"the place was shaken wherein they were gathered together; and they were all filled with the Holy Spirit, and they spake the word of God with boldness." Now here is something else. The whole place was shaken. That was later on; there was an earthquake. *That* never happened again. So you have three things here. The first day the symbol was that of a sound and that of a sight, the sound of the wind, the sight of fire disparting; and just a little later on in the history the shaking of the whole house, the earthquake. These were *all* immediate things, incidental, not essential, and never repeated according to these records.

You know, I never read about these things and group them without remembering Elijah. Do you remember, when Elijah was waiting for God, what happened? There was a wind, and the Lord was not in the wind; and there was an earthquake, and the Lord was not in the earthquake; and there was a fire, but the Lord was not in the fire. Then, to put the Hebrew into straight English, there came the sound of a solemn stillness, and that was God. Now, I do not want to overemphasize that, but I always go back there when I get into the Acts. Here you have it—symbols. The sound of the wind, the sight of the fire, the tremor of an earthquake. But God was not in the sound of the wind, nor the sight of the fire, nor the tremor of the earthquake. The *fact* was a silent stillness; they were filled with the Holy Spirit. *That is the great fact.*

My brethren, perhaps I need not say it to you, and yet I am going to say it, and I say it with great love and respect. People who are trying to get back to a shaking house, and sound of wind, and sight of fire, and tongues of that sort are missing the value of all these things. They are symbols, arresting attention at the dawn, and never repeated. We shall have to come back to that in another application a little later on. But we can see how wonderful it was to them; the sound of the wind in the house, filling it, rushing over the city so that the whole city was arrested by that sound, God's act. Inside, fire disparting, and *it*, the one fire, sat upon each of them and took the form of a tongue—the tongue which was to be the instrument of their work, for they were to be witnesses; the tongue, which forevermore was to stand as the symbol of the Church's activity.

The tongue has three functions—praise, prayer, prophesying; and by prophesying I do not mean predicting. Predicting is a secondary element in prophesying. Prophesying is speaking forth the Word. The tongue is for praise, for prayer, for prophesying, and the fire shadowing the real thing is the emblem and the symbol of it. And what an emblem! What a symbol! Do you notice that the emblem of fire is used with regard to the tongue for both good and evil? Has that ever occurred to you, I wonder? When I name it you know what I am referring to now. Let me turn to it for a moment. I turn to the epistle of James. Go to the third chapter and notice these words—I am reading at the fifth verse. "So the tongue also is a little member, and boasteth great things. Behold, how much wood is kindled by how small a fire!" The literal translation of that is, "Behold, how great a forest is set on fire by a small fire." Now listen. "And the tongue is a fire: the world of iniquity among our members is the tongue, which defileth the whole body, and setteth on fire the wheel of nature, and is set on fire by hell"; and hell there is not Hades, it is Gehenna.

So your tongue is set on fire by hell—or what? Well, go back here to the sixth chapter of Isaiah only for an illustration: "In the year that King Uzziah died I saw the Lord. . . . Then said I, 'Woe is me, for I am undone'. . . . Then flew one of the seraphim unto me, having a live coal"—a burning coal—" . . . and he touched my mouth with it, and said, 'Lo, this hath touched thy lips; and thine iniquity is taken away, and thy sin forgiven.' " The tongue is always on fire either of heaven or hell. You see the symbolism of the fire and the tongue. These people in the upper room saw the tongue. That is what they alone were given to see. They were not to go out and use the weapons that are carnal in their warfare. They were to use the tongue for praise, for prayer, for prophesying.

Then in your reading you come to the supreme fact; "they were all filled with the Holy Spirit." We leave that until we come to our next study.

You say, Why are we stopping? Because the time is gone. . . .

CHAPTER 2

ACTS 2:4

We ended the previous study with the expression, "they began to speak with other tongues," and there the same word for "tongues" means "languages"—they spake with other tongues, or languages, as the Spirit gave them utterance.

Now we started by saying that in this little paragraph we have the account of the birth of the Christian Church. On that great day the day of Pentecost was fulfilled then and there, and we dealt with the suggestive accompaniments of the essential fact. We did not deal at length with the last, and I am going to postpone it further—the gift of tongues—because when we get down into the next paragraph we have the description of that as it came from the lips of the men of the city. You remember: "How hear we, every man in our own language wherein we were born?"

Today I want us, as we may be helped by this selfsame Spirit, to consider the thing that happened that day which is *central* and *essential*. What was it? "They were all filled with the Holy Spirit." This is the supreme word in the record. The sound of the wind, the sign of the fire were symbolic. Divinely chosen and appointed, and therefore not to be omitted. Only they were transient. They never heard that sound again so far as the Acts of the Apostles records. They never saw that sign again so far as the record tells us. They did—in the fourth chapter, you remember, have another sign. The Spirit came with a new manifestation, and the whole house was shaken; so that you have the wind, and the fire, and the earthquake. And we dared to go back to Elijah's experience when he was looking for God. And God was not in the wind, and God was not in the fire, and God was not in the earthquake, but He was in the sound of gentle stillness.

Further, that speech with tongues (to which we will return later, because I think it very important for us to understand what the New Testament teaches about the gift of tongues) was a gift of ecstatic utterance. The gift of tongues was never bestowed for preaching. These men were not preaching. They were praising. Now, that *was* repeated, and when you get on to Paul's letters you will see what he thought about it. So that you and I need not be at all perplexed about the gift of tongues. There it is—an expression, a very remarkable one, but not particularly valuable as Paul points out. He says he would rather speak five words with the gift of prophecy than talk with tongues.[1] All I want to say to you now is this: it was an expression of the central fact. What was the central fact? "They were all filled with the Holy Spirit."

So now let us settle down just with that one statement. The verb here is a simple and a sublime one, meaning exactly what it says—they were filled. You will find this word is used figuratively, and translated in other ways in other places. It is a word that suggests being imbued, supplied, furnished. Yet all of these break down, and there is nothing better to carry over the idea in our tongue than the word "filled." What *is* important for the Bible student to understand is this: here you have a word that describes an *act,* not a condition. "They were filled with the Spirit" does not mean to say only that they were full of the Spirit. They *were* full of the Spirit, but the emphasis of the declaration is upon the *act,* the experience of the

29

moment. Do not let anyone misunderstand me. Of course it means they became full. If you are filled you become full. But let us get clearly in our minds the whole meaning of the great declaration, "They were filled with the Spirit." They were caught up *in* the Spirit. They were penetrated *by* the Spirit. They were brought under the *power* of the Spirit.

You remember how in those last discourses of Jesus, or shall I say those intimate and wonderful conversations of Jesus with His disciples in the upper room—you have often noticed it, I only go back to it to refresh your memory—He said, "I will inquire of the Father (or I will pray the Father), and He shall give you another Comforter." [2] There is a word I always wish had been allowed to go out into our English language in the actual word used here, "another Paraclete." It is too late now because it would puzzle a lot of young folk, and yet we don't get all the meaning in the word Comforter. Another word you get sometimes is the word Advocate. Well, yes, you want both of them. If you put the two words together—Advocate, Comforter—you have two interpretations of His work. The word Paraclete, meaning One called to the side of another, is the great word. Our Lord said, "He shall give you another Comforter, that He may be with you forever, even the Spirit of truth, Whom the world cannot receive."

In those same conversations He said that the Spirit would convict the world. Oh, yes, the Spirit comes to the world. The Spirit was poured upon all flesh as well as upon the Church. "Whom the world cannot receive; for it beholdeth Him not, neither knoweth Him. Ye know Him"—listen to this; this is what I am after, "He abideth with you and shall be in you." It is that word *"in"* that is the great word in that declaration. He abideth with you, He shall be *in* you; and *this* was the day when *that* thing happened; "They were all filled with the Holy Spirit." Then and there they were born again of the Spirit of God, and that birth meant that they came into a new life in every way. Straightway they had a new consciousness of their Master, a new consciousness of themselves, a new consciousness of all things. Life was completely changed to them in that moment.

If I use mechanical terms I do so in order to arrest and fasten attention. Within an hour after that coming of the Spirit they knew Jesus better than they had known Him in all the three and a half years they had been His companions. They were born into an entirely new consciousness of Him. They had been through a wonderful experience.

How they loved Him in those days when they were His disciples! Yet in some senses, while He was with them He was always outside them, and Himself limited, "straitened." That is His word—you can drop the word limited, but take His own—"straitened." There were things He could not do. But they loved Him; and you know how when they saw Him put on the Cross, all their hope perished. Their faith did not fail. Jesus prayed for them that their faith should not fail. Later, talking to Simon, you remember He said this, "Simon, Simon, behold, Satan asked to have you" (*plural—all* of you) "that he might sift you as wheat; but I made supplication for *thee*" (singular).[3] That does not mean that He had not prayed for the rest, but He was dealing with this one man. He had prayed that their faith should not fail, and it did not. Peter's faith did not fail when he denied his Lord. His courage failed but not his faith. And his love never failed. The disciples' love for their Lord never failed in those darkest days when they saw Him done to death and put on the Cross; but their hope failed.

You remember the two going to Emmaus, what they said? When Jesus joined Himself to them in that wonderful way, hiding Himself when He was near them—that is what he could do, so that they did not know who He was; and He looked at them and said, "What communications are these

31

that ye have one with another, as ye walk?" And they looked at Him in surprise. "Are you a lodger in Jerusalem, and do not know the things that have happened?" [4] And He said, "What things?" Don't you just love that story, watching how He drew the men out? Now listen to them: "Jesus of Nazareth, Who was a prophet mighty in deed and word before God." They believed in Him and loved Him. But wait a minute. "But we hoped" (past tense) "that it was He who should redeem Israel." That is what was dead—their hope. And Peter, when he came to write his letter says, He "begat us again unto a living hope by the resurrection of Jesus Christ from the dead." [5]

Hope was born again by the resurrection, but not understanding. *That* had not come. And that is why He told them to tarry, to do nothing until they received this gift of the Holy Spirit. It was not hope that was renewed with the coming of the Spirit, but it was understanding that came to them. They were "filled," they had a new consciousness, I repeat, of their Master, of themselves, of all things. Their outlook on life was completely changed. It was the daybreak of Christianity as an experience in the world. Until that moment there had been no Christianity except Christ Himself. He had never been able to complete His work in the case of the souls who were nearest to Him. It was then, when they were all filled with the Holy Spirit, that the thing happened.

Handling this quite reverently, let us think of what that event meant in relation to the work of Christ; and then, secondly, what it meant in the experience of these men.

Now let me answer the first question: What did it mean in relation to the work of Christ? I suggest, to begin with, that this was the culmination of the earthly mission of the Son of God, and the commencement of His heavenly mission which was made possible *through* the earthly mission. May I repeat that in general terms. That day, in that upper chamber, when the Spirit of God came as He had never come to humanity before, when He came and filled that group of souls, when they were filled with the Holy Spirit—that was the culmination of His earthly mission; and it was the commencement of His heavenly mission *consequent upon* the completion of His earthly mission. His heavenly mission, yes. He has entered into heaven itself, and He is still working. But all He *does* is the result of what He *did;* and in that hour you have the culmination of His earthly mission.

Now I am going back for a moment. We are conscious, of course, of the difference between the earthly work of our Lord and the Acts of the Apostles. I do not mean by that that our Lord's message to men was changed. Not at all. Some people tell me that in the days of His flesh He preached the Kingdom and then abandoned it. I differ absolutely from that interpretation. There is a sense in which it is perfectly true that the Kingdom of heaven as an established order on the earth is postponed; but the ideals are not, and the Church is still responsible for interpreting them to the world. But there *is* a marked difference.

Now you have noticed (and I am only refreshing your memory) how Luke begins this story, and the significant word is a little word that we are very likely to hurry over. I go back to chapter one, verse one. "The former treatise I made, O Theophilus, concerning all that Jesus began both to do and to teach." Now, I read that for years, and did not notice it. I read it accurately, and thought about it inaccurately. I am sure you are constantly waking up to the fact that you have been reading a thing accurately and thinking about it inaccurately. I read that, or thought of it as though Luke had written, "concerning all that Jesus did and taught." Oh, no! It says, "all that Jesus *began* to do and to teach." *Began.* Keep your mind on that for a moment for we are just comparing. I am turning back now to the third chapter of the Gospel according to

Luke, and in that chapter he says at the twenty-third verse, "And Jesus Himself, when He *began,* was about thirty years of age." Now you have your Bibles open. Do you not have two other words in there—"to teach"? I am reading the Revised Version: "Jesus, Himself when He began to teach, was about thirty years of age." But the words "to teach" are supplied, for they are not in the Greek text. Those who were translating thought they must fill up the gap, so they put in "to teach." Well, it is wholly wrong, and it is not complete; and if I want to fill in the gap, I go back to Luke's second treatise and use the words "to do and to teach." The whole point is this, that when I read that in the third chapter of Luke, unquestionably at that point he was referring to our Lord's earthly mission. Now after you have read all the story of His teaching and working of wonders, His Cross and resurrection and ascension, you have got everything. But when Luke begins his second treatise he says, "The former treatise I made . . . concerning all that Jesus *began* both to do and to teach." What is the patent inference? That He did not finish, that He had something else to do and teach. Well, where do I get the record of that? The first part of it is in the whole of the Acts; that is the key to the Book of the Acts. The Book of the Acts is the first chapter of how Jesus *continued* to do and teach through His Body, the Church. That is the real title of the book.

Now you see the incompleteness of the first story, and the beginning of the completion of it in the second.

Now there is something else, and again I am going back to Luke. Here is a very wonderful little paragraph in the twelfth chapter. Neither Matthew, Mark or John have recorded it, and yet how full of pregnant suggestiveness it is. We are in the story of the life of Jesus, and one day, in the midst of His teaching and public utterances, He, the Lord, broke out into what I am constrained to call a cry, a soliloquy. A great cry that came out of His heart. It is not so much something he

34

said to the crowd, though the crowd heard Him. He was talking to them just before and after. But suddenly there came
this great cry, and this is it. He said, "I came to cast fire upon
the earth; and what do I desire? Would that it were already
kindled!" [6] Remember, that does not mean, What would I do
if it were already kindled, as though the Lord were suggesting
He came to cast fire, and what would He do if He found the
fire already kindled. No, it is just a sigh, a sob. It came out
of his soul, His desire. "I came to cast fire on the earth, and
what do I desire? Would that it were already kindled! But I
have a baptism to be baptized with, and how am I straitened
till it be accomplished!" I need not insult your intelligence by
telling you that it was not the baptism of Jordan, for that was
long past. It was the passion baptism to which He referred, the
baptism in death, the mystery of the Cross. He said He came
to cast fire on the earth. "And what do I desire?" What is the
consuming passion of my life? Would that that fire were already kindled! But it cannot be. I have a baptism to be baptized with, and how am I straitened till it be accomplished.
Now I turn over into the Acts of the Apostles, and I find this
same Lord Jesus on the other side of that passion baptism, and
He is no longer straitened. He now *can* cast the fire, and that
is what He did on the day of Pentecost. The fulfillment of the
earthly mission and its completion is accomplished when this
thing happened, and the Spirit was cast upon men.

May we stand reverently behind this little paragraph as we
are trying to find what this meant in relation to the work of
Christ, and speak of the work of the Son of God for humanity.
First there was a heavenly service, and then an earthly service,
and then a heavenly service. Whether the word service is the
proper one for the first, I am not quite sure. There was a
heavenly activity before there was an earthly one. Then came
the process of the earthly one and the completion of that, and
the commencement of the heavenly one.

What was the heavenly one before the earthly? We go to the second chapter of Paul's letter to the Philippians for that. "Who, being in the form of God, did not count His equality with God a prize to be snatched and held for Himself, but emptied Himself, and took the form of a servant." [7] There is the heavenly transaction.

The light is too bright
For the feebleness of a sinner's sight.

I never really begin to apprehend the profound meaning of that until I watch Him on earth; but I never understand the earthly activity until I see it linked with that heavenly transaction. That passage in Philippians, "Who, being in the form of God . . . emptied Himself." That is the first thing.

Then what is the last thing, completing it, before a new, a heavenly ministry can begin? "They were all filled with the Holy Spirit." "*He* emptied Himself"; "*they* were all filled with the Holy Spirit." There are great boundaries there. "He emptied Himself" functionally, not essentially. It does not tell us that He laid aside His Deity. There is nothing to warrant that in all our New Testament. I have a few of my brethren here in the ministry, and they will understand me when I say, Don't you think it is time we gave the Kenosis theory a little rest, and gave more attention to the Pleroma? We have heard so much about the Kenosis and about that passage. It is there. That is where it all began, the Kenosis, the Self-emptying. But when next you are going to give a course of sermons on the Kenosis, link up with it your Colossian letter, with its passage on the Pleroma. "It pleased the Father that in Him should all the fulness dwell" [8] corporeally. You have got your Kenosis, but you have also got your Pleroma; self-emptying, but abiding fulness. Of course, if you are going to use the Shorter Bible you do not find that passage on the Pleroma. They have cut it out! I am not dwelling on controversial matters, but there are some things that make a man angry who loves his Bible. I am quite free to say that the Shorter Bible makes me angry. It is the latest illustration of spiritual ignorance masquerading in the garb of supposed learning.

Very well, where were we? That Self-emptying in which he divested Himself, not of that which was essential, but of functional activity. He stooped from the exercise of sovereignty to the exercise of submission. He consented to be conceived of the Holy Spirit, and He consented to live under the mastery of the Holy Spirit. The Holy Spirit led Him into the wilderness. Full of the Spirit He did *all* He did. He was Servant, Self-emptied. We tarry with very deep reverence around that great passage; and I say as I end my contemplation of it, I cannot interpret Jesus save in the light of that fact; and the moment you begin to do it you have lost the Christ of the New Testament, and the Christ of the Christian Church, and the Christ of God.

There was the heavenly activity—the Self-emptying; then the earthly—the fact of the Incarnation, God manifest in flesh; then the ministry of word and work—He went about doing good—through which ministry God was interpreted and man was interpreted; this is the great interpretation. And then the infinite mystery of the Cross wherein and whereby He did bear away the sin of the world. And then the stupendous wonder and victory of the resurrection, God's demonstration of the perfection of the Man, and the victory of His passion. And then what? The ascension. What does that mean? It means that the risen Jesus went up into heaven itself. Now, you believe that there is a heaven somewhere; your New Testament teaches you that. Jesus of Nazareth ascended. He was not dissipated into thin air in that moment of ascension. If that were so, then your New Testament is inaccurate from beginning to end, and the whole scheme is false.

There "at the right hand of the majesty on high," [9] is a Man of your humanity and mine, the Man of Nazareth. So I watch Him. "He emptied himself . . . being made in the likeness of men"—that is incarnation; "and being found in fashion as a man"—that leads you to the transfiguration, when he came to the full height of His human nature. "He humbled Himself," He left the mount and came down to the valley and took His way to the Cross, and became "obedient unto death, yea, the death of the Cross, Wherefore God highly exalted Him"—resurrection and ascension—"and gave unto Him the Name which is above every name." Exalted to the right hand of God, He returned to the fellowship with the Father in the sovereignty that He had laid aside for the earthly course; He returned to the activity of God with the Spirit; and *then* He poured out that gift upon those waiting souls. It was the completion of the merciful and majestic and mighty movement— God in Christ, from the heavens, through earth, back to the heavens. He emptied Himself and then He filled those waiting souls; they were filled with the Holy Spirit. For the experience that He was able to give to them in that way, there is no other word than this: they were filled.

Here let me tarry for a survey of the technicalities of the passage. You will find in the New Testament that the relation of the Spirit of God to the believer in Jesus Christ employs that word over and over again—"they were filled." And you will find three other terms used: baptism, anointing, sealing. Three terms, not four; the one filling interpreted. The filling was the baptism; the filling was an anointing; the filling was a sealing. Now at your own leisure take out all the places where you find filling, baptism, anointing and sealing, and you will find no intermixture. The baptism means a death into life. I am not talking about the rite of baptism just now, but remember that the rite is very eloquent in itself, and the rite of baptism always symbolizes death, and life unto death, and through death into life. But I am not concerned here with the rite. I am concerned with the *fact* of which the rite is the symbol; and the baptism of the Spirit is that wherein men pass from death to life. It is not a "second blessing." Now I am not quarreling with you if you say that you have had a second blessing. If you mean that you have been living for years on a certain level and have passed to a higher level of life, I am sure that is true of thousands of Christians. In the New Testament baptism is never used of a second blessing. It is regeneration, renewal. It may be that a man does not apprehend all he gains in his regeneration, and it may be that scores and hundreds have entered, years after, into a larger meaning of apprehension, and they have had a second blessing, mightier than the first; but when they were baptized by the Spirit they were born again. Baptism is always regeneration.

I know that this is a controversial subject. You say, Were not these men born again before? Certainly not, in the New Testament sense. Was not Abraham born again? No, not in the New Testament sense. The Christian Church is a separate thing. Abraham received the Divine gift, the Divine life, and he received it on the basis of the Cross, for the Lamb was slain from the foundation of the world. But the Christian Church is a separate entity, and that is something that we have to recognize right here; and that little group of disciples was born again *then,* never before.

Now someone will say, But did not the Lord say to them after His resurrection, in the upper room, "Receive ye the Holy Spirit"? He did, but they did not receive Him then. That was prophetic, for afterwards He said, "Now tarry until you are endued with that power." The Spirit came at Pentecost, and the filling of the Spirit was a baptism, death into life, and an anointing. And wherever you find the word anointing it indicates not so much the passage from death into life but rather fitness and power for service.

Go back into your Old Testament, and find anointing. Who were these who were anointed? The king was anointed, the priest was anointed, the prophet was anointed; and all Messianic references are to One Who should be anointed as King, anointed as Priest. "The Spirit of the Lord is upon Me, Because He hath anointed me. . . ." [10] Anointing simply indicates that the baptism whereby men were born again is also equipment for service. Anointing marks that. Sealing is the same thing, but might have another phrase there in another relation. Sealing is the sign of a covenant. On that day when the Spirit filled them they were baptized from death into life, they were anointed for all the service to which they were appointed, and they were sealed, and the sealing was a covenant. It meant that they were wholly at the disposal of God, and that God was wholly at their disposal. They entered into a solemn relationship with Him, a covenant, and that was the culmination of the great work of the Lord.

Here we are, among the Lenten shadows. Presently we will come to Palm Sunday, and we will tread Holy Week with reverence until we come to the hour of the crucifixion. We will rejoice with our lilies at Eastertide, and then we nearly always forget—now, forgive me, you Episcopalians, for *you* do not, but *we* often do—Ascension Day. You may have some idea that there is a Whit Sunday, but you do not take much notice of that either. Someone says, We do not notice it at all. I am not saying you must. There is no law in this matter. My temperament is that I always observe these special days, and in my church in London we missed no festival of the Church. It is curious how you all love Easter! Well, Ascension comes forty days after Easter, and then Pentecost (Whit Sunday) ten days after Ascension. Just as I love the feasts of the Lord in the Old Testament as giving me the calendar of God, so I love these festivals of the Church as giving me the calendar of redemption.

Let us go over that again from the other standpoint. What

was the *fact* in the experience of the disciples? What happened when they were filled with the Holy Spirit—what really happened? What difference did it make? In that filling, that group of men and women were joined to the Man at God's right hand in one actuality of life. Oh, beloved, how can that be said so as to bring all the wonder and the power of it back to the consciousness of the Christian Church! What is Christianity, after all? What makes me a Christian, or you a Christian? Admiration of the ideal of Jesus? Well, let me speak respectfully to you. You tell me you are a Christian because you admire Him. I do not understand you. My admiration for Jesus as an ideal fills me with the uttermost consternation because I fall so absolutely short of it. The ideal of Christ is held up before me, and I am told to copy it, and so be a Christian. If you tell me that you are laughing at my impotence, mocking my paralysis, not having understood the deep, deep need of my sinning heart and soul, that does not make me a Christian. It may make me an admirer, but the very admiration reacts in despair if that is all. Well, what is it to be a Christian? It is to live one's life with the risen Lord by the Holy Spirit. Said Paul, "He that is joined unto the Lord is one spirit," [11] and I do no violence to the great declaration if I put it in another form—he that is filled with the Spirit is joined to the Lord. Those men and women in the upper room —no wonder people thought they were drunk presently! But more of that by and by. That little group was filled with the Spirit; they were living one life with the risen Christ. They began to see as He saw, to feel as He felt, to know as He knew.

"He that is joined to the Lord is one spirit." In Him and in us the Spirit dwells, moves and manifests Himself. In that hour Peter, James and John were brought into vital, actual, living union with Christ. That is what He meant when he told them that it was better for them—I will take the old word if you like—"it is expedient for you that I go away; for if I go not away, the Comforter will not come." [12] Let us look at the historic fact. While He was there with them He was so near that John could put his hand on Him, and I name John because he said he did it. He says, "That which we . . . handled." [13] John could touch Him, and Peter could look clean into His eyes. I say that because we are told that Jesus looked at Peter and Peter was watching Him. When Peter was betraying his Lord, Jesus looked at him. Wonderful, was it not? Did it ever occur to you that if Peter had not been looking at Him, he would not have seen that look? He was a long way down, but he had his eye on Jesus still. Yes, they could listen to Him and handle Him, and yet He was outside them and they were outside Him. But that day when the Spirit, proceeding from the Father through the Son, came and filled them, the beating, pulsing power in Him and in them was one. *That* is Christianity. And you and I are Christian men and women if we are living one life with the risen Son of God. "They were all filled."

What does that mean? With great reverence go back over the ground of the work of Jesus, and see how that coming of the Spirit linked those men and all who believed on Him with those things which are told about Him. He emptied Himself. Why did Paul say to the Philippians, and so to us, "Have this mind in you, which was also in Christ Jesus: Who, being in the form of God, did not count His equality with God a thing to be grasped, but emptied Himself." [14] "Have this mind in you. . . ." Now that is what the Holy Spirit does first. He brings us into the place of self-emptied men and women. That is what the Lord meant when He said, "If any man would come after me, let him deny himself." [15] Who says that? The One Who had emptied Himself. That is what it meant at Pentecost. That group of men and women, when the Spirit came and filled them, became self-emptied. How wonderful it was! Oh, they had their failures and breakdowns, but the main truth about them is that they were self-emptied souls. That is also the main truth about every man who is born again.

Yes, but if He emptied Himself and came into this world, what did He come for? To manifest God. That is what the filling of the Spirit means. If we are Spirit-filled we shall go out, wherever we live, to reveal God. Man, I tell you, it pulls a man up! It makes him ask how far he is resisting the Spirit, or quenching the Spirit, or grieving the Spirit. That is what Peter meant when he wrote his letter. Hear the words again. "Ye are an elect race, a royal priesthood, a holy nation, a people for God's own possession, that ye may show forth the excellencies of Him Who called you out of darkness into His marvellous light." [16] And as Christ was the unveiling of God, your bodies become temples of the Holy Spirit; and in proportion as that is so, you are revealing God in Christ wherever you go.

And as He, revealing God in His Person, served humanity, so do Spirit-filled men and women in word and in work forever serve. The Son of Man came not to be served but to serve, and to give His life a ransom for many. The Body of Christ, the mystical Body, the multiplication of the One by the one hundred and twenty, by the three thousand, by the four thousand, by the millions, is not in the world to be ministered to, but to minister. Service becomes the very law of life.

Yes, but where did it lead Him? It led Him to the Cross. Where is it to lead us? Right there. Not for our own salvation now—that is where we started out. But for fellowship in His sufferings, that we may make up that which is behindhand in the afflictions of Christ.[17] That is what the filling of the Spirit means.

Anything else? Oh, yes. Where did He go? Having offered Himself through the eternal Spirit, He was raised. And if I am filled with the Spirit He brings me into fellowship with Him in the deathless life, already into the realm of resurrection.

And where next? To the right hand of the Father reigning. And the filling of the Spirit means that we are seated with Him in the heavenly places, reigning; reigning over forces, reigning over circumstances, never mastered by them but reigning over them.

And what was the last thing in the mission of Our Lord? He poured out the Spirit. What about us? Well, let Him tell you, He said one day, on the last day of the feast of Tabernacles, "If any man thirst, let him come unto Me and drink." That is the first thing. "And he that believeth on Me, as the Scripture hath said, from within him shall flow rivers of living water." [18] And John adds, "This spake He of the Spirit." And in proportion as that is so, from us the living streams are flowing to others. It was a great day, that day of Pentecost.

Now may I amend that and say that the day of Pentecost in that sense is still here. *This* is the day of Pentecost. *That* was its dawning. *This* is the age of the Spirit. The Spirit was no more in that upper room than He is with us now, in this church. We do not see any tongues of fire. That was incidental, and is not necessary for us or it would be given. We hear no sound as of a mighty rushing wind. That was merely symbolic. But the Spirit is with us if we are His. "But if any man hath not the Spirit . . . he is none of His." [19]

Well but, you say, what is the matter with us? And then somebody says, What we need is more of the Spirit. No, my friend, God bless you, do not say that again. If you want to say something that is true, do not say we need more of the Spirit. I will tell you what it is: The Spirit needs more of us. We are holding back some part of the territory. You say, We are waiting for the Spirit, we have been waiting long. Oh, no. The Spirit is waiting for us, and since that moment when you and I were born of the Spirit, baptized, anointed, sealed, we have allowed some of the channels to become clogged, we have shut up some of the territory of our beings, we have excluded Him, we have not yielded to Him. The moment we open the doors, He flows in.

I used to sing a hymn which said,

> My all is on the altar,
> I'm waiting for the fire.

I do not sing that any more. Why not? Because I do not think it is true. I will tell you what I *might* have sung,

> A part is on the altar,
> I'm waiting for the fire.

The moment all is there, the fire is there. "They were all filled with the Spirit."

Now just this last word. These symbols of the Spirit are very suggestive—the symbols that our Lord used. If you go back to the Gospels you will notice that He used three there. He used the wind, He used water, and He used fire. He used the wind as a symbol: "The wind bloweth where it will, and thou hearest the voice thereof, but knowest not whence it cometh, and whither it goeth: so is every one that is born of the Spirit." [20] He used water as a symbol: To the woman He said, "Whosoever drinketh of the water that I shall give him shall never thirst; but the water that I shall give him shall become in him a well of water springing up unto eternal life." [21] And in the seventh chapter of John to which I have already referred, "He that believeth on Me, as the Scripture hath said, from within him shall flow rivers of living water," and John adds, "This spake He of the Spirit." [22] He used fire as a symbol: "I came to cast fire on the earth," and His herald, John the Baptist, had said, "I indeed baptize you in water

. . . He shall baptize you in the Holy Spirit and fire." [23] There is a whole line of study there, and I think it would be one of profitable devotional meditation when one is alone.

The wind—that is the element of life, supremely. You can live longer without bread than without water. How long can you live without bread? You can live something like six weeks without food. How long can you live without water? Not nearly so long. How long can you live without breath? How many minutes? The wind is the element of life. That is one figure of speech.

The rivers are always the emblem of satisfaction and renewal. Satisfaction—a spring of water, laughing up into life. As to renewal, go back to Ezekiel, where is the river that came by the way of the altar, and under the threshold; and the great word concerning it, wherever the river came there was life. [24]

Fire always stands for two things in your Bible: energy and purity. Those are Christ's symbols. That is enough. Think them through; and notice this; whether you take the wind, or water, or fire—what are they? They are forces which are mighty and yet mysterious, all of them forces capable of destroying life. Get into cyclone country and let a cyclone strike you. Or be out in the ocean when the wind is at work. Wind, water and fire can destroy life; but they are all things necessary to life. You cannot live without any of them, *but* you have to discover their laws and obey them. If you obey them they bless you. If you disobey them they blast you. So is everyone that is born of the Spirit. It is a terrible thing. It is a glorious thing; and what you and I have to do is to obey the law of the Spirit, and then the Spirit within will fulfill all the Divine purpose. If I break that law, that selfsame Spirit will work unto my death, and not to my life.

Take your figures again. As to the wind, what am I to do? Live on the heights and breathe it. Do not go back into the malarial districts. As to the water, live in the stream of it. Do not go to a Bible Conference just to get filled up. That is one of the most mistaken ideas in the world. A man in England says, "I am going to Keswick to get living water." The moment you have water in a vessel it is not living, it is stagnant. Living water is always water flowing in and out. You cannot store things up that way. As to the fire, live in the fire and do not quench the fire. I am only passing over these figures of speech.

"They were all filled with the Spirit." Are we? We certainly were when we became Christian men and women. That is what made us Christian. Are we today? If not, why not? That is a question that cannot be answered by any one person for another. Now do not forget that. The writer of the letter to the Hebrews charged us to lay aside every weight, and the sin that doth so easily beset us. What is the weight? Anything that stops you running. I will tell you one weight. Trying to find out what your brother's weight is. Lots of people are busy on that business. I do not know what is preventing the fulness of the Spirit in any man's life but my own. All right. Our business is to see to it that, in our own lives, we unclog the channels, open the windows and doors, and let the Spirit have His way with us. Then, through us, •God will be seen, and the work of Christ will be accomplished.

CHAPTER 3

ACTS 2:5-13

Let us turn once more to the second chapter of the Acts of the Apostles. I am going to read verses 5-13.

Now there were dwelling at Jerusalem Jews, devout men, from every nation under heaven. And when this sound was heard, the multitude came together, and were confounded, because that every man heard them speaking in his own language. And they were all amazed and marvelled, saying, Behold, are not all these that speak Galilaeans? And how hear we, every man in our own language wherein we were born? Parthians and Medes and Elamites, and the dwellers in Mesopotamia, in Judaea and Cappadocia, in Pontus and Asia, in Phrygia and Pamphylia, in Egypt and the parts of Libya about Cyrene, and sojourners from Rome, both Jews and proselytes, Cretans and Arabians, we hear them speaking in our tongues the mighty works of God. And they were all amazed, and were perplexed, saying one to another, What meaneth this? But others mocking said, They are filled with new wine.

We come now to the third of our meditations in this wonderful chapter. We notice in the verses I have read to you, the first impression made upon the outside world by this thing that took place.

Let me say first that the whole Book of Acts divides itself quite naturally into the movement of these early Christians, this Christian Church constituting the new, the mystical Body of Christ, out into the world. In chapter one our Lord gave them the program. "Ye shall be my witnesses" you remember, "in Jerusalem, and in all Judaea"—you see the circles getting wider—"and Samaria," and then the final sweep of His compass, "and unto the uttermost part of the earth." And the whole book of the Acts follows that line.

For the first seven chapters they are in Jerusalem. Then Luke gives a brief record of how, by persecution, they were driven out; they went through Judaea preaching the Word. Then, driven forth, they went over into Samaria, and at the end of chapter eight he tells how they moved toward the uttermost part of the earth. First toward Africa—Philip and the Ethopian eunuch; then presently, by the apprehension of Saul, out toward Asia; and then later on, when Paul saw the beckoning finger of the man of Macedonia, toward Europe— the uttermost part of the earth—and your story ends right at the heart of the known world, with Paul in Rome.

Chapters one through seven are full of interest because they reveal the first things in the history of the Church: the first impression made upon a city, the first message delivered,—to that we are coming—and beyond what we look at in these studies, the first opposition to the Church, then the first practice of the Church's communistic fellowship, then the first fiery discipline—Annanias and Sapphira, and the first definite persecution. Then came the first organization when the deacons were appointed, and then the first martyr—all first things through seven chapters. I have gone a little aside because that brings us back to the verses, which we have read together— Acts 2:5-13.

Here we see the first impression made. We are going to look at two things. First the impressive facts, the things that produced the impression; and then the impression made by those facts. Luke here, with very great care and accuracy, tells us exactly the impression that the early Church made upon the city of Jerusalem.

Now while we are studying this chapter together, let us look for its spiritual values. So we go back again to the beginning. We are among the hills where the springs are bubbling up that become the great rivers of God. We may test our own condition by this backward look. We are not called upon to reproduce anything accidental or incidental, but we *are* to discover the essential values of all these things. We are going to examine these verses to see the impression the Church made upon the city of Jerusalem; and all the way through we must ask ourselves whether the Church of God is making its impression on the city in which we live. I am not going to answer that inquiry for you because I cannot. I do not live where you do, and I do not want anyone to answer it for anyone but himself. Let us who name the Name and profess to belong to this Church of God go back and ask, When the Church was born, what was the first impression made upon the city? That is our theme.

Well now, if we look at the impressive facts, we notice first, things that we can only name as supernatural. The city was impressed first by a startling sound, "a sound as of the rushing of a mighty wind," and that brought them together. Notice how Luke tells it: "When this sound was heard." In the Authorized Version it reads, "Now when this was noised abroad." It is quite right—only you do not live in the year 1611! You are saying, What do you mean by that? I mean that in 1611, when this translation was published, and they read "was noised abroad" they understood what it meant. Today the impression of the reader is that the story of the thing became a rumor; it was rumored, it was noised abroad. That is how we use the expression now. It did not mean that in 1611. So we read, "When this sound was heard." What sound? "Sound" does not mean a rumor, a report. It means exactly what it says— a noise in that sense.

Now, says Luke, "When this sound was heard, the multitude came together." So there was a supernatural sound which the whole city heard. Luke has already told us that it was a sound from heaven, so that the city heard a sound as though it was rushing down towards them from heaven. And it settled at one point. Where did it settle? On the place where these people were assembled. So that it was the supernatural element which first impressed the city.

Someone says, Yes, I read that, but of course I don't believe it. Well, I am not going to argue with you, my friend. I can only say to those who tell me that, Why don't you believe it? Because, they say, we do not believe in anything supernatural. Well, there we part company. I am afraid I cannot help you very much. But remember, supernatural things are only supernatural to you and to me, because we do not understand them. There is nothing supernatural to God; and this declaration that there, at the beginning of the Christian movement, there was some action of God whereby through a sound he attracted a city, is to me perfectly rational, perfectly easy of belief.

Now then, wait a minute. Someone says, But why don't we get that now? It was incidental, it was valuable then and there. You and I may think it would help us a great deal *now* if God would make a noise and come down on top of the building. That is where we are wrong. If it would help, God would do it. That is the whole thing. You and I have to see from the very start that God is doing the right thing all the while; and the moment you and I begin to hanker after something that is spectacular and supernatural, we are missing the value of this story. What God does is always necessary. It was necessary *then*. Let us make a note of that in our minds.

Now the next fact: The multitude found this group of people, quite possibly having come out of the house—and this is speculation. (Now, remember what I said about that. Never take any notice of a speculation when a man is preaching or teaching.) It may be that they were moving out onto the roof, or it may be that they came out into the street. One thing is certain. They were not in the house, because you cannot put three thousand people into any ordinary house. The probability is that these people came out, and when the city gathered round them, there was the most amazing fact. What was it? The fact that this company of men and women were speaking or chanting or singing in all the languages that were represented in Jerusalem at that time. And Luke tells you here that there were dwelling at Jerusalem—and the word means that they were dwelling temporarily—devout men, Jews, from every nation under heaven. It was the feast of Pentecost, and Jerusalem was crowded with Jews from all over, as they came up to the feast. And they found these people, in many languages and many dialects, with perfect distinctness and clearness, showing forth the mighty works of God.

Now here is the point where we may naturally and properly stay to examine this gift of tongues; "tongues" now being used of the languages these people were uttering. We are going to stay a few minutes with it because you and I know, beloved, that it *is* a subject of interest, if that is the right word. It is well for us to go back and see what the Bible has to say on that subject. Again, I am not going to stay arguing as to whether this thing ever happened. You have another thing here that is distinctly supernatural. You have a group of Galileans for the most part, (as the crowd said: "Are not all these that speak

Galileans?") You know what lay behind that. They meant comparatively unlearned and unlettered men. "How hear we, every man in our own language wherein we were born? . . . we hear them speaking in our tongues the mighty works of God." That the crowd heard that, there is no manner of doubt. Here is something supernatural, something not to be accounted for in any other way.

These people were speaking in many languages, but what were they saying? I want to impress upon you first that they were not preaching, they were not addressing the crowds; or if I may use the other word which is an accurate word, they were not prophesying. What were they doing? They were praising God, but doing it in all the languages that were represented there. That was a supernatural activity of God, the Holy Spirit, through these people for a certain purpose. But it is a fact, and what they were doing was of value.

Now I want to say to you that the gift of tongues *is* here in the New Testament, recognized here, referred to twice more in the Acts of the Apostles and dealt with very definitely by Paul in his Corinthian letter. In order that we may have the facts quite positively in our thinking, let us turn to the passages.

I turn first to the tenth chapter of the Acts, and read from verse forty-four:

> While Peter yet spake these words, the Holy Spirit fell on all them that heard the word. And they of the circumcision that believed were amazed, as many as came with Peter, because that on the Gentiles also was poured out the gift of the Holy Spirit. For they heard them speak with tongues, and magnify God.

You know where Peter was at the time. I need not go back. But this is typical of the narrow misapprehension that charac-

terized Jewish believers at the beginning. They had great difficulty in getting away from the idea that this was not for them
alone.

" . . . They heard them speak with tongues, and magnify
God." You see that again they were speaking with tongues,
and what were they doing? Magnifying God. Compare it with
the declaration in the second chapter," . . . we hear them
speaking in our tongues the mighty works of God."

Turn now to the nineteenth chapter in the book of Acts and
the sixth verse. Paul had come to Ephesus and found there a
group of people who believed in Jesus. But something impressed
Paul, something different, something lacking. You remember
how they had come to be believers in Jesus. It had been the
result of the ministry there of Apollos. And Paul said to them
in the second verse, "Did ye receive the Holy Spirit when ye
believed?" Do get that. Did you hear what I read? Paul did not
say, "Have ye received the Holy Spirit since ye believed?"
There is no single passage that I know of in the Acts of the
Apostles that has misled more people than that translation in
the Authorized Version. That is a palpable error made by the
King James translators. Paul said, "Did ye receive the Holy
Spirit *when* ye believed?" which is quite a different matter.

Now listen to what they said, "Nay, we did not so much as
hear whether the Holy Spirit was given." And that word
"given" is a supplied word. They said in effect, "We did not so
much as hear whether there was any Holy Spirit." Just imagine! Paul asked, "Into what then were ye baptized? And they
said, Into John's baptism."

Now do not be confused here. These people at Ephesus had
believed, but not into the fulness of the Gospel of Jesus the
crucified and risen Saviour. They only knew what had been
told them. Apollos, when he began to preach, was preaching
only what he knew of Jesus through John the Baptist, until a
man and his wife, Aquila and Priscilla, took him aside and

fully instructed him. But these Ephesian people simply k
what John had preached. That is why they had not rec̲.
the Holy Spirit. "And Paul said, John baptized with the baptism of repentance, saying unto the people that they should
believe on Him that should come after him; that is, on Jesus.
And when they heard this, they were baptized into the name of
the Lord Jesus." Now listen. "And when Paul had laid his
hands upon them, the Holy Spirit came on them; and they
spake with tongues, and prophesied." Here are two things;
they are not the same. They spake with tongues. They prophesied. Two gifts—do not confuse them.

Now these references show that the gift of tongues, whatever
it was, was a gift enabling those who had it to praise God, and
not necessarily in marv languages. On the day of Pentecost it
was in many languages, but the gift of tongues was something
beyond that. It was a gift whereby the soul was lifted into the
high realm of perfect ecstasy and devotion and adoration, and
poured itself out in praise to God. That is what the gift was
for, and on that occasion in Jerusalem it was done publicly.
And the city gathered about and heard people praising God in
every language represented there.

What about that gift of tongues today? Is there such a
thing? And if there be, what have we to do? You have all your
instructions in the New Testament, and you will find them in
the fourteenth chapter of I Corinthians. It is a subject altogether too great to go into a detailed interpretation here, but
we can see quite clearly the instruction concerning the gift of
tongues in the Christian Church.

Now, you cannot begin your reading in I Corinthians at the
fourteenth chapter. Everyone who studies it knows that perfectly well. The moment you get down to study you will find
that chapters are a nuisance, and that they often begin at the
wrong places. For instance, in this fourteenth chapter you
have no business to begin, "Follow after love." That is a bit of

the thirteenth chapter. Notice how the thirteenth ends, "Now abideth faith, hope, love, these three; and the greatest of these is love. Follow after love." Do you see that I am reading from one chapter into another, straight on?

Very well then, if I am going to understand chapter fourteen and all it tells me about the gift of tongues, I must know what is in the thirteenth. What is in chapter thirteen? Everybody knows. But thirteen does not begin with the first verse of the chapter. You and I have no right to begin there: "If I speak with the tongues of men and of angels, but have not love, I am become sounding brass. . . ." That is not where Paul began. Go back into the previous chapter and in the last verse, you read, "But desire earnestly the greater gifts. And moreover a most excellent way show I unto you. If I speak with the tongues of men and of angels, but have not love. . . ." You see, chapter thirteen belongs to chapter twelve, and chapter fourteen belongs to chapter thirteen, until we go back—how far shall we go back? Go back to the beginning of chapter twelve, for that is where Paul began the second part of his letter.

You know the movement of this great letter to the Corinthians. First you have eight verses in chapter one, all introduction. Then, in verse nine Paul says, "God is faithful, through Whom ye were called into the fellowship of his Son Jesus Christ our Lord." That is the fundamental proposition, and everything in the letter has to do with that. You are called into the fellowship of the Son of God. God called you there, and God is faithful. On the basis of that fundamental proposition, where is the final appeal? The last verse of chapter fifteen: "Wherefore, my beloved brethren, be ye stedfast, unmovable, always abounding in the work of the Lord, forasmuch as ye know that your labor is not vain in the Lord."

Now you take your Corinthian letter sometime and just work it out for yourselves. Look at it; study it. Introduction, eight verses. An illustrated finish—chapter sixteen, and a conclusion, for he is talking about all sorts of people and sending messages to them. The great argument of the letter lies between verse nine of chapter one, and verse fifty-eight of chapter fifteen. Did you ever take those two verses together and see how they fit? "God is faithful, through whom ye were called into the fellowship of his Son Jesus Christ our Lord. . . . Wherefore, my beloved brethren, be ye stedfast, unmovable, always abounding in the work of the Lord, forasmuch as ye know that your labor is not vain in the Lord."

These are the boundaries. What is between? Two movements. The first movement is corrective. Paul is dealing with the carnalities of the Church, the things that separate from Jesus Christ in service. As a matter of fact, Paul wrote this letter in answer to one he had had from them. You have noticed that. This letter is an answer; only Paul, with fine spiritual art, said things they did not ask. He never gets to his answer to them until the seventh chapter: "Now concerning the things whereof ye wrote. . . ." But he had said a good deal before he got there. What had he dealt with? Divisions in the Church—that is the first thing. Some said, I am of Paul; and some, I am of Apollos; and some, I am of Cephas; and some, I am of Christ—and do not forget that that too was a sect. The people that said, We are of Christ only, were just as much a sect as the others. Divisions!

And when Paul had dealt with that he turned to another matter—moral derelictions in the Church. They were permitting immorality, unjudged. And when he had dealt with those two things he said, Now, concerning what you wrote about, and he dealt with their difficulties in social relationships and all sorts of things; and when he got to the end of chapter eleven, you remember his last sentence, "And the rest will I set in order whensoever I come."

They must have been in a bad state in that Corinthian Church. Do not forget that when you tell me the Church is in bad shape today. I defy you to find anything worse than that Corinthian Church, according to this letter. And when Paul had dealt with those carnalities, he said, "Now, concerning spiritual gifts"—no, that word "gifts" has no right there. The Greek word is "pneumatikon," it is a plural word, and you can only render it by saying, "And now concerning the spiritualities." He has been dealing with the carnalities; now, he says, "concerning the spiritualities."

Now, beloved, we have gone a long way to get to the fourteenth chapter. I do not apologize for that. More and more I feel we only see the meaning of a section when we get a conception of the whole. What are the spiritualities of the Church? The unity of the Church first. As the first carnality was divisions, so the first spirituality is unity. You remember: "There are diversities of gifts, but the same Spirit." It is in the chapter about the unity of the Church and the diversity of its gifts. At the end of chapter twelve he says, "God hath set some in the Church, first apostles, secondly prophets, thirdly teachers, then miracles, then gifts of healings, helps, governments, divers kinds of tongues. Are all apostles? Are all prophets? Are all teachers? Are all workers of miracles? Have all gifts of healings? Do all speak with tongues? Do all interpret?"

Quite evidently they did not, and all were never intended to. God gives gifts as He will, says the Apostle. Notice that the gift of tongues is named. "But," he says, "desire earnestly the greater gifts." That is what he is leading to. "And moreover a most excellent way show I unto you." What? The most excellent way of desiring gifts. What is the principle of desiring gifts? He continues, "If I speak with the tongues of men and of angels"—that is a higher reach than you and I know anything about—"but have not love, I am become sounding brass, or a clanging cymbal." I need not read more. You know it. But what is the principle of desiring gifts? That is what he is after. Love. And he celebrates love in that classic passage;

and immediately he says, "Follow after love." That is the principle. "Yet," he says, "desire earnestly the spiritualities, but rather that ye may prophesy."

Now, here is a wonderful thing. In chapter fourteen he takes two gifts, the gift of tongues and the gift of prophecy, and he contrasts them. He says, in effect, that the gift of tongues is not to be compared with the gift of prophecy. The gift of tongues has its place and its value. We will glance at some of the statements. There *is* such a thing, declares Paul, and he says, I have it. I speak in tongues more than any of you; but, he says, "I had rather speak five words with my understanding . . . than ten thousand words in a tongue." Let us glance down the chapter and see what he says.

In verse two, "He that speaketh in a tongue speaketh not unto men, but unto God." Well, that is what I was saying to you about the gift in the Acts. They were not preaching, they were not speaking to men, they were speaking to God. That is a great thing.

Now look at the fourth verse. "He that speaketh in a tongue edifieth himself; but he that prophesieth edifieth the Church." Now, the edification of self spiritually is not a bad thing. It is a good thing. Paul says *that* is the value of the gift of tongues. If a man has this gift, it is not one that enables him to talk to men, but to God; and in doing that, he is finding edification. It is the life of the soul above the place that is commonplace, where it adores and worships, and in a great, high ecstasy praises God. Oh, he says, it is good. You are edifying yourself by doing that, but you are not edifying anyone else. Mark his distinction. Look at the fifth verse, going right on, he says, "Now I would have you all speak with tongues, but rather that ye should prophesy: and greater is he that prophesieth than he that speaketh with tongues, except"—now then mark this—"except he interpret, that the Church may receive edifying." He says if a man has the gift of tongues and uses it, the people will not know what he is saying. He is in a high altitude of spiritual worship, which is strengthening to his life; but if the gift is exercised in the Church there must be someone there to interpret, so the Church can understand.

Glance on again at verses seven to nine. I want you to notice this carefully. He says, "Even things without life, giving a voice, whether pipe or harp, if they give not a distinction in the sounds, how shall it be known what is piped or harped? For if the trumpet give an uncertain voice, who shall prepare himself for war? So also ye, unless ye utter by the tongue speech easy to be understood, how shall it be known what is spoken? for ye will be speaking into the air."

Do you notice that every one of Paul's illustrations here is a musical one—pipe and harp, the trumpet and the voice—all the way through? The gift of tongues is for praise. Now, he says, if you have that gift and are exercising it, you are not helping other people; consequently the gift of tongues is not the supreme gift. Now on the day of Pentecost there were people of many languages to hear, and *there* was the value of it; but, says Paul, in the ordinary run of the Christian life of the Church that will not be so, for you would not be understood.

Verse twelve: "So also ye, since ye are zealous of spiritualities, seek that ye may abound unto the edifying of the Church." The passion that makes you desire gifts is not to be for the gift that blesses *you,* so much as for the gift that will help you to bless someone else.

He illustrates this again in verses fourteen to sixteen, and presently, in the eighteenth verse he says, "I thank God, I speak with tongues more than you all." I never come to that without stopping to think that there I may have some little insight into the private life of Paul in his adoration and worship. When Paul was away from the crowds, away from the saints, when he was alone, praying, and having the gift of tongues, he was lifted above even the limitation of the languages he knew. And he knew more than one. He knew the Latin tongue, the Greek tongue, the Hebrew tongue, and the Aramaic tongue. And yet there were moments when he was lifted up, and his language was above them all. I have it, I have it more than all of them, he says. "Howbeit in the Church"—in the assembly—"I had rather speak five words with my understanding, that I might instruct others also, than ten thousand words in a tongue."

You see where he puts the gift of tongues. Yes, you say, there *is* such a gift. Is there a value to others? Look at verse twenty-two. "Wherefore tongues are for a sign, not to them that believe, but to the unbelieving."

Now you are back in Acts 2. On the day of Pentecost tongues were a sign, and the sign was to make people inquire. Tongues were for them. Tongues may have that value still. Paul says in effect, If you have the gift of tongues, it is to make people inquire. Now here are the instructions, verse twenty-three: "If therefore the whole church be assembled together and all speak with tongues, and there come in men unlearned or unbelieving, will they not say that ye are mad? But if all prophesy, and there come in one unbelieving or unlearned, he is reproved by all, he is judged by all; the secrets of his heart are made manifest; and so he will fall down on his face and worship God." You see that Paul says here that even the gift of tongues as a sign is not as valuable as the gift of prophesying.

All right, go further on to verse twenty-six. "What is it then, brethren? When ye come together, each one hath a psalm, hath a teaching, hath a revelation, hath a tongue, hath an interpretation. Let all things be done unto edifying." That is your principle. Very well. "If any man speaketh in a tongue" —what then? "Let it be by two, or at the most three, and that in turn."

Now I want you to observe how very definite and even mechanical Paul was. Supposing, he says, you have in your midst a man who has the gift of tongues, or two or three men, let only these speak, and let them not do it together but in turn. All right, but wait a minute. "But if there be no interpreter, let him keep silence in the Church; and let him speak to himself, and to God." There you have it. There is a man who says he has the gift of tongues. There are two. Take them in turn. Is there someone to interpret? No. Then they cannot do it here; they must go home and do it.

Then he went on to the other gift, the gift of prophesying. There you also have clear instructions. When you reach the end of the chapter, verse thirty-nine, he says, "Wherefore, my brethren, desire earnestly to prophesy, and forbid not to speak with tongues. *But let all things be done decently and in order.*"

I do not think there is any subject under heaven on which you have more careful instructions than that. And the thing that happened on the day of Pentecost was that a company of people with the first experience of the Spirit, found themselves lifted up, praising God, and doing it in many tongues. But remember, there were people of all tongues present, and it was a sign to *them;* but the gift of tongues was of no value to that crowd beyond amazing and perplexing them and making them critical. Peter had to get up, and in the gift of prophecy explain. There was the great place of preaching to which we are coming.

Well, you say, what are your applications of all this to us and to the present day? My brethren, I do not need to make them—they are all there. You know that at certain points here in the United States, and in England and other places, great interest is taken in this matter of tongues. All right, I am not objecting to it. I am perfectly sure that the gift of tongues can be bestowed. But when it is bestowed—supposing it is bestowed here, where we are. We know exactly what to do according to Paul's instructions. One at a time may speak, but not without an interpreter. If there is no interpreter, go and use the gift at home. Perfectly simple.

Now I have something else to say to you. Did you ever take the New Testament and make a list of all the gifts—the gifts of the Spirit? Paul makes a list once or twice. Notice that he never makes the same list twice over. You will find that the Spirit bestowed gifts then that He does not bestow today; and you will find that He bestows gifts today that He did not bestow then. Go back to the great statement of the paragraph in Acts 2:4: "They were all filled with the Holy Spirit, and began to speak with other tongues, as the Spirit gave them utterance." The gifts that were given at the beginning were not necessarily to be continued through all the ages. What *is* to be continued? *The Spirit, and the Spirit filling the church.* That has never been changed. And that Spirit will bestow the gifts. Go back to the twelfth chapter of I Corinthians at your leisure, and you will find it in the unity of the body: ". . . but all these worketh the one and the same Spirit, dividing to each one severally even as He will." [1]

The Spirit of God bestows upon a man the gift of healing. I am ready to acknowledge it. That can be done. It has been done. It was done in the early Church. I think it has been done since. Indeed, I think I know a man upon whom God has bestowed the gift of healing today. He does not argue with you that faith is necessary. He comes and lays his hands on you, and heals. You say, why does not God give that gift to every Christian? That is His business, not yours. He divides "to each one severally even as He will." When He bestows the gift of tongues, I am ready to believe it, but I would like to say this: Personally, I have never found the gift of tongues yet. I have been in places where they said they had received the gift, and they were unintelligible either to the next man or to the man himself. I am not denying it; but it is a secondary gift in value, according to the apostolic teaching, and the laws for its observance are laid down very stringently because of the peril of it. Some may yet have it. All right, let them fulfill the conditions; exercise it in public if the interpreter is there to interpret to the group; otherwise, let him go home and exercise his gift of tongues there.

It was bestowed upon this group at Pentecost, and the thing I want to stress above all is this: It lifted them into the highest place of adoration and praise. Oh, men and women, my brothers and sisters, would to God we had something of it in some form, more powerfully than we have! I do not mean the gift of tongues in language, but "the garment of praise for the spirit of heaviness." [2] Has it not occurred to you how little we know, even in the worship of the Church today, of pure praise? You test it. Take your own hymnbook, I do not care what hymnbook it is, and go through it, and see how many hymns you can find in your book of pure praise. I do not mean prayer. Prayer is not praise. I do not even mean thanksgiving. Thanksgiving is not the same as pure praise. Praise is adoration of God for what He is in Himself, and for what He has done, not for me, or you but for what He is. And you know, I think perhaps if some of us knew more of the gift of tongues exercised in spiritual power, we should know more of the tongue of praise, not in unintelligibility, but in force when we get together! At any rate, here is your first view of the Church, the Church on fire, their eyes flashing, their faces radiant with joy, and on their lips praises to God. In their case they were expressing these things in all the tongues, because God would arrest the attention of all who were gathered together in Jerusalem at that time.

Luke tells us that the multitude "came together, and were confounded," and in the seventh verse he says that "they were all amazed and marvelled"; and he brings everything together in the final declaration in the twelfth verse, ". . . they were all amazed, and were perplexed, saying one to another, What meaneth this?"

They were amazed. What does that mean? Mental arrest, not yet illumination. As they saw and heard these people they did not understand it, but they were arrested, they were filled with wonder—and wonder is the origin of worship. Worship does not always succeed wonder, but worship never begins apart from wonder. Here you have a city amazed, intellectually arrested, and compelled, at least for an hour or so, to forget everything else—their commerce, their homes, their schools, and their discussions. They were amazed at what they saw and heard. A Church amazing a city!

But they were not only amazed, they were perplexed. If amazement means mental arrest, perplexity means mental defeat. They could not explain it. There is no illumination in perplexity. They knew they did not know.

What next? Inquiry. "What meaneth this?" Now is the preacher's chance. That is when Peter began to preach. That crowd did not come to hear Peter, you know. Peter was not a popular preacher drawing a crowd. The crowd was drawn by the Church. It was the Church on fire which attracted the crowd, and when the crowd was amazed and perplexed, they cried, "What is it all about?" *Then* Peter got up and began to preach. (In our next study, we shall see what he had to say under those circumstances.)

But last of all, they were critical. They made one guess, as far as I know. That is all Luke has recorded as the only attempt to solve the mystery of the Church: They are all drunk! They said, "They are filled with new wine." They were not so far wrong. They were just as far wrong as heaven is from hell, and no further. When Peter began to preach—I will just go as far as that—the very first thing he said was, "These are not drunken, *as ye suppose.*" If you want to think it out intelligently, listen to Paul, "Be not drunken with wine, wherein is riot, but *be filled* with the Spirit." [3]

What is the value of it all to us? These things, the sound and the speech in many languages, were initial and incomplete, requiring prophecy to produce results. Signs are always secondary. They have their place and value, but they never carry anyone anywhere without prophetic interpretation. So far as we are concerned, may I suggest these concluding thoughts to you. Put the incidental in its proper place. The Spirit-filled Church always presents to the world supernatural phenomena, producing amazement, perplexity, criticism. No church is doing its work unless it is doing something supernatural that cannot be done anywhere else. Go through the Acts. Things happened. A lame man was healed, you remember. Presently the apostles were miraculously released when they were locked up—another supernatural manifestation. They had a new fellowship, and that was so new that many in the city wanted to join them on that basis. Then two people inside that communion violated its principles, and swift death overtook them; and the world outside saw that, in that community, there was a fiery discipline that did not allow a liar to live; and again the supernatural had its effect. Presently, what? I am picking things out all through the story. Stephen died. Nothing supernatural in that? No. But look at his face; listen to his prayer; and notice that one clean, strong, cultivated, clever young Jew there, who never got away from the look on dying Stephen's face. He tried to drown his conviction by persecuting Christians until Jesus said to him, out of the brightness, "Saul, Saul, why persecutest thou Me? it is hard for thee to kick against the goad." [4]

And so you go on and on, all the way through—not always supernatural things in our little sense, but always something in the Church that is not found anywhere else. And unless the Church is producing results that cannot be produced anywhere else, she is failing. They can educate in the schools. They can amuse elsewhere, but the Church of God must be producing supernatural results in the spiritual realm, in the moral realm. Do not let us waste time hoping we shall see fire, or a cyclone. Those are transient, unimportant things. But the Spirit-filled Church is producing phenomena that will make the outside world amazed, perplexed, critical. Our business is to be so Spirit-filled that He may be able to produce the new phenomena that *our* age requires.

Oh, this Church of God! How we love the Church!

> I love Thy Kingdom, Lord,
> The house of Thine abode,
> The Church our blest Redeemer saved
> With His own precious blood.

How we have blundered, and how we blunder yet! Our anxieties have been false. We have been so anxious that emperors should patronize us. That has been the story of the past—a blighting story. We have been so anxious to be established by the State. In the United States you know nothing about that now. You got away from that when, in New England, you burst the bonds in one particular Church. I remember a spiritual snobbery in my own land. I hear it yet—Well, we are getting on wonderfully. There were ten carriages at our Church door yesterday morning! Anxious about that? Anxious about our theologies, anxious about our organizations! The one anxiety should be that we are in such fellowship with the Spirit of God that we are a Spirit-filled people of life, and light, and love, and liberty, with fire and fury against evil—a Church on fire! That is what brings the crowds together, and they say, What is the matter with these people? That gives the preacher his chance.

We shall start there in our next study, and see what the preacher did with his chance.

CHAPTER 4

Acts 2:14-47

We have made reference to the first impression made upon a city by the Christian Church. We noted the words of Luke, "They were confounded . . . amazed . . . perplexed." They said to one another, "What meaneth this? But others mocking said, They are filled with new wine." We saw the impression made by this Spirit-filled company of men and women, new light in their eyes, the rapture of an entirely new life sweeping them into this great service of adoration, the service of the tongues and the city watching.

We are told that they were amazed. I repeat that that means mental arrest. That is the first impression that the Spirit-filled Church had upon the city. They were perplexed, and that means mental defeat, inability to explain the thing that has arrested them. And that led, quite naturally, to the inquiry, "What meaneth this?" And some said mockingly, "They are filled with new wine."

Now, this impression created the opportunity for the preacher. Let us get hold of that. There is a whole philosophy in that statement. A Spirit-filled Church will always amaze the world and stir the outsider into saying, "What meaneth this?" and that presents the opportunity for preaching.

We come now to the first sermon ever preached in the history of the Christian Church. First we are going to look at it in a general way, and then consider it in more detail in the next four studies.

The opportunity for preaching is what I want to stress first, and it came when the city was made to inquire into the meaning of what they saw in the Church. That is very important, and may God help us to grasp its meaning. I am speaking now to officers and members of all Christian churches. In proportion as the churches fulfill the ideal set forth at the beginning of this chapter—in that proportion will your preacher have a better time preaching.

I am sometimes told that preaching today is on a lower level than it used to be. That is a subject I would like to discuss at some length. First of all I would have to say, I do not know, I have not much opportunity of judging. I do not hear preachers very often, but I would like to say this: I never miss a chance, when I can, to hear preaching, and at least ninety-nine sermons out of a hundred that I hear, get to my soul and help me. I do not find preaching on a low level. There is a great tendency, you know, to contrast the preachers of today with the preachers of yesterday. If we only had so-and-so back again! Well, I'd like them to come back and have a try. I don't know. But supposing it is so, that preaching is not on a very high level today, generally speaking; I will tell you one reason it is not, and only one. It is that the Church is not giving the preacher very much to explain. There is a good deal of action and reaction between preaching and hearing, between the pulpit and the pew. You give me a Spirit-filled Church with an inquiring crowd asking, What is the matter with these people? and your preacher has the biggest chance to go out and explain. That is what Peter did. That is the place of real preaching, when we are interpreting the life of the Church, which has arrested the community.

Today we have another idea. We think the work of the

preacher is to get the crowd. There is a classic story told of a request in a letter written to Charles Haddon Spurgeon, who was, at that time, the head of the Pastors' College: "Can you send us a preacher who will fill our church?" Spurgeon wrote back: "No, that is not a preacher's job to fill a church. I will send you a man to fill the pulpit; *you* fill the church." He was perfectly right. Peter was not announced throughout Jerusalem. There were no newspapers, no pictures of Peter to get the crowd. All these are modern additions. The Church on fire, the city inquiring, and then came the preacher's chance. That is what the second chapter of the Acts says to me.

In the whole of that which remains we have an account of the first message delivered, and of the results which followed the preaching. This study, then, reveals the true method of preaching, the subject matter of preaching, and the results that followed the preaching, And all that is so important that we are going to take time to work our way quietly through it. We are going to examine a sermon and its results.

In this study I want us to survey the sermon as a whole, to see the general movement of it and watch the method. We shall have to read it bit by bit as we go through, so I will not stay here to read it in its entirety.

Beginning at verse fourteen: "But Peter, standing up with the eleven, lifted up his voice, and spake forth unto them, saying. . . . " That is the introduction. Then begins the actual message, "Ye men of Judaea, and all ye that dwell at Jerusalem, be this known unto you. . . ." and so on to the end of the discourse.

I am taking for granted your general acquaintance with it, and the fact that you have your Bible open in front of you and can notice certain things. There are three things to be observed: the physical things that are worth note; the mental things which will hold us a little longer; and the spiritual things which are supreme.

You say, What do you mean by the physical? Let us read it again: "Peter, standing up with the eleven, lifted up his voice, and spake forth unto them, saying. . . ." That is all.

If I were lecturing to students in a theological seminary I would stop with that a long time. The statement is very simple and suggestive. Notice first that when Peter delivered this sermon, he stood up. Did you notice that? "Standing up." Did that ever impress you? You young folk, reading your Bible, did you notice that? You say, Of course he stood. But that was something quite *new*, and Luke draws your attention to it. Standing up was a new attitude for preaching. The rabbis all sat down; Peter stood up; and immediately you are introduced to a fresh element in preaching. Jesus had told these disciples before He went away that they were not to be called rabbis.[1] That does not mean that they were not to be teachers, because He sent them out to preach and teach. But it is significant when on that day on which the first sermon was preached, Peter adopted a new attitude to address the crowd. Instead of sitting down, he stood up. Sitting was the habit of all teachers, preachers and prophets. Indeed, Jesus sat to teach. He delivered His great Manifesto sitting. You remember how Matthew 5 begins: "Seeing the multitudes, He went up into the mountain: and when He had *sat down*, His disciples came unto Him. . . ."

But on this day of Pentecost something new happened. Peter stood up. Now, a man who stood to address a crowd was always a herald. He had some authoritative proclamation to make. It may have a teaching value in it, but it is the attitude of the herald. My brethren in the ministry will be familiar with what I am going to say next. There are two great words that describe preaching in the New Testament. As a matter of fact there are eight or ten different words, but there are two supreme Greek words, and I am going to name them. One is the word "euaggelizō," which means to preach the Gospel, to tell the good news. Then there is another word, "kērussō," which always means to proclaim as a herald. It indicates the attitude of one who represents a throne, and is delivering a message of full and final authority. Peter stood up that day, not to suggest that the teaching element is to be absent, but to show that the Christian preacher *stands* always to speak with authority. If he does not, he is not a Christian preacher. I do not mean to say that he may not be a Christian man, and dealing with a Christian subject. But preaching means delivering a message from God. That is fundamental. If I come to you to discuss some subject about which I am inquiring, and which we are investigating, and on which I am proceeding along the line of a hypothesis, that is all right, but it is not preaching. Peter stood as a herald. It was a new attitude, and though I may seem to be straining after a word, I am doing nothing of the kind. If you had been in that crowd in Jerusalem, you would have noticed the attitude immediately; instead of sitting down to talk, he stood.

There is another thing which I am not going to be dogmatic about, but here it is: It says, "standing up with the eleven. . . ." Not only did Peter stand, but the eleven stood with him. I am not going to suggest that my brethren in the ministry stand round while I am preaching; but it was a remarkable thing, and it was a manifestation to that crowd. One is speaking, but all the rest are round about him in the same attitude. It is the sense of authority that fell upon them with the message they were to deliver.

Now the next thing need keep us only for a moment, but we will notice it: "Peter lifted up his voice. . . ." If I were talking to students in a theological seminary I would say more on that point. You see, he had at least three thousand people to reach, perhaps more. And if a man has to reach three thousand he must not speak as though he were addressing thirty. We will consign that to the lectures on homiletics, but it is important.

Another thing. He "spake forth." What does that mean? It simply means that his enunciation was clear, not merely in the articulation of his voice, but in all the method of his presentation. He "spake forth." You get that verb, or rather that idea —the cognate word—in the Acts of the Apostles three times.[2] You have it twice here in the second chapter. In reference to the tongues, "They were all filled with the Holy Spirit, and began to speak with other tongues, as the Spirit gave them *utterance*"; and the word "utterance" is the noun cognate with the verb "to speak forth." The Spirit gave them clearness of articulation even while they were speaking in tongues. You will find it again in the twenty-sixth chapter. Paul is before Agrippa, and Festus says to Paul, "Paul, thou art mad; thy much learning is turning thee mad." And Paul says, "I am not mad, most excellent Festus; but *speak forth* words of truth and soberness." [3] That is, I articulate clearly, and what I am saying is stated with clarity so that it may be understood. You see the value of these little things as we are reading. He stood up; he lifted up his voice; he spake forth.

One other little word. "He spake forth *to them*." Well, why put an emphasis there? Because again you have what preaching is. Preaching is never speaking *before* people, it is always speaking *to* people. A man who is discussing a subject in the presence of a crowd and talking before them, is not preaching. He may be doing good work, but it is not preaching. The preacher talks *to* his people.

A little while ago, in a ministerial conference in England, a minister said that, when he was a boy, preaching consisted in a combat between the preacher and his congregation. He was fighting them in the sense of wooing and winning them. He was compelling them, by argument and illustration, in the power of the Spirit, to decisions—not only decisions for Christ but decisions all along the way. And he added that that day had gone. I do not think he was quite right there, but the measure in which his statement was true is the measure in which the preacher may be failing today. The true preacher is always speaking *to* people, and always bringing men to decision, not only to decision for Christ but to decision in accordance with the truth proclaimed. Any man who is simply preaching to defend his own orthodoxy is breaking down. Unless you and I have the moral and spiritual intent and make our appeal to the will, we are failing. "He spake unto them," and you will find that before Peter got through he made his appeal directly, and called them to act in accordance with the things he had declared.

Now those are the little things, if you like, the incidental things, but it is impossible to pass them over. He stood up, he lifted up his voice, he spoke forth with clear enunciation, both as to his words and as to the statement of his facts, and he spoke unto them. A wonderful little verse about preaching.

Now, if you have your pencil and don't mind making little marks in your Bible, I am going to ask you to mark one word at certain points in the narrative. It is the word *"this."* Let us look at certain strategic points. In verse twelve you read, "What meaneth *this?*" At the end of verse fourteen you read, "Be *this* known unto you. . . ." Then in verse sixteen it says, . . . but *this* is that." Put a mark under these words. Now go on down to verse thirty-three and you will find "he hath poured forth *this*. . . ." Mark that word. I know this is quite technical, but don't be afraid of it. Four times the word is used. Have you marked them all? Do you see where they are? The crowd said, "What meaneth *this?*" Peter said, "Be *this* known unto you." He then said, *"This* is that," and at the end he said, "He hath poured forth *this.*"

The first thing I want to stress is that the whole sermon was a recognition of the right of these people to inquire, and it was an answer to their inquiry.

The people said, "What meaneth this?" Peter said, "These

are not drunken, as ye suppose; seeing it is but the third hour of the day"—and that was the hour of sacrifice, and no Hebrew drank anything until that was over. "Be this known unto you. . . . this is that. . . ." What does he mean? He means, You have asked this. I will explain this. He is going to interpret the thing they had looked at. Then, when he had introduced his theme, speaking of their false suggestion that they were drunk with wine (and keep your mind on what these crowds were looking at—people all aflame, the shining eyes, the songs), he said, "This is that which hath been spoken by your prophet." And he quoted Joel's prophecy. And if you want sermon divisions, that is the first division of Peter's sermon. It ends with verse twenty-one.

Now when he had done that, he started again: "Ye men of Israel, hear these words: Jesus of Nazareth, a Man approved of God unto you by mighty works and wonders and signs which God did by Him in the midst of you, even as ye yourselves know; Him, being delivered up by the determinate counsel and foreknowledge of God, ye by the hand of lawless men did crucify and slay. . . ." So he continued, and told them of His crucifixion, told them of His resurrection, told them of His exaltation. And at last he said, "He hath poured forth *this.*" Do you follow his message? Do you see his method?

To go back once more: "What meaneth *this?*" "Be *this* known unto you." *"This* is *that"* which your prophet said should come. Jesus of Nazareth "hath poured forth *this.*" Peter said, "Be *this* known, . . ." There are things you need to know about it. First, you ought to have expected it. It is in fulfillment of your own prophetic literature. Secondly, it has happened through the Man you crucified, Jesus of Nazareth. What is this? Go back to your prophet and you will know. How did this happen? Keep your eye upon Jesus of Nazareth and you will know. We are getting at the scheme, making notes of Peter's sermon. Remember all the time that the whole of it is based upon the recognition of the right to inquire; it is an answer to their inquiry.

The preacher began by interpreting on the plane of their knowledge, of what they *did* know. Two things they knew. They knew their own prophecy, or ought to have known it. The probability is that they were familiar with their prophet. Peter began right there: *"This* is *that* which was spoken by your prophet."* You see, he led them on the line of the realm of the thing they knew. Then, "Jesus of Nazareth, a man approved of God unto you . . . as ye yourselves know," he said in effect. You ask the meaning of what you see in these people. Now, he said, there are two things you know. You know your prophets, and you know about this Man Jesus who was living among you recently. You know all He did. You know the wonders and the signs. You know about Him. The two things you *do* know, rightly apprehended, will explain the thing you do *not* know.

Here is another profound thing about preaching. First, you must always recognize the right of the outside man who wants to know the meaning of the things produced in the life of the Church; and the business of the preacher is to interpret those things. Secondly, the true preacher always begins on the level of the things men know, and sets these in relation to the great facts of revelation. Any missionary will agree with me. When you go out to the heathen world you do not go out to abuse, you go out to find the element that is there of knowledge, and then to bring to bear upon it the great Word of God, fulfilling the element that is true. Paul on Mar's Hill— where did he begin? He quoted from their own poets, and took one of their own altars. Someone says that he failed on Mar's Hill. Nothing of the kind! Let us get rid of that idea. A great expositor, years ago, gave that as his view, and it seems to have possessed thousands of readers ever since. He said that when Paul went to Corinth he said to them, "I determined not to know anything among you, save Jesus Christ, and Him crucified"; and that Paul meant, I tried a different method at Athens and it failed, so when I got to Corinth I determined that I would know nothing save the crucified Christ. Now that is the most implausible exegesis I ever saw. Because Paul did *not* break down at Athens; when he said, "I determined not to know anything among you, save Jesus Christ, and Him crucified" [4] he did not mean that that was *all* his message. It was not all his message. If you want all his message it is this, "It is Christ that died, yea rather, that is risen." [5] He said, I could not talk to you about the positive side of Christianity. You were carnal, so I had to keep you in the realm of the Cross. He was not contrasting the Corinthians with the Athenians. My brethren, the only reason some people think Paul failed in Athens is that the statistics were not very good. Only a certain woman named Damaris, and Dionysius the Areopagite and a few others believed. You do not fail if your statistics are not good; some of the biggest statistics being exalted in this land and elsewhere will be proved to be failures. You cannot judge spiritual results by counting heads. If you go outside the New Testament and look at the later history of the Corinthian Church, and the Church at Athens you will find that the Church at Athens was a living power long after the Church at Corinth. Out of the Church at Athens came Basil and Gregory and others of the great fathers of the Church.

However, let us get back. I have not lost my way! When Paul went to Athens he began with them where they were, and when he got up yonder to Lycaonia, he did not begin as he did in Athens. He began with Jupiter, and put him into contrast with Jesus. My dear friend, Dan Crawford, who went to the long grass in Africa, found that the natives have a fetish worship. He did not laugh at their fetish, but began to interpret the deep necessity that underlies it, and then put Jesus where the fetish was. So Peter, beginning his preaching, starts with the things they know. You know about your prophet; you know about Jesus of Nazareth. Now put them into relation with each other.

Then again, when he had quoted the prophet—and if you want to be ready for the next study, read the prophecy of Joel all through—how very wonderful is the orderly statement of truth that fell from his lips! He began, "Ye men of Israel, hear these words: Jesus of Nazareth. . . ." Now go to verse thirty-six, ". . . God hath made Him both Lord and Christ, this Jesus Whom ye crucified." He takes them all through the mystery of His life and His death and His resurrection and His exaltation and Lordship; then ends, ". . . this Jesus Whom ye crucified."

Now notice one thing more in the mental method. Three we have looked at: first Peter recognized their right to inquire, and responded to it; secondly, he appealed to the things they knew and based his argument on them; thirdly, he put the truth in an orderly form as he stated it. Finally, what? Go right to the end and see what he says: "Let all the house of Israel therefore know assuredly. . . ." *Know assuredly!* It is the bringing of all the argument to the climax, to the personal appeal. "Let all the house of Israel therefore know assuredly, that God hath made him both Lord and Christ, this Jesus Whom ye crucified." The last thing is the definite and authoritative proclamation of that man who stood—not sitting as a rabbi, but standing as a herald—preaching a sermon in which he related the thing that caused the inquiry to their own prophetic utterances, and then related that same thing to the history of Jesus of Nazareth. The last thing is the final proclamation that God hath made that Jesus both Lord and Christ.

Very well then, if you go over this discourse and consider it no longer from the ground of the physical and the mental, but of the spiritual, it becomes even more interesting and wonderful. First notice Peter's immediate response to the Spirit and his obedience to the Spirit in the witness he gave. I am sure you have often thought of the change wrought in this man by the coming of the Spirit. We all know what a courageous coward he had been. Is that a fair definition? He had always had a lot of courage, this man, but he had been an awful coward too. He began with the phrase, "Jesus of Nazareth," and don't forget that that name was absolutely hated by the rulers. They had flung Him out, this Jesus of Nazareth. Yet, in obedience to the Spirit, Peter bore this testimony in Jerusalem. He had no position, no precedence, no power, no influence behind him. There he is, standing up, and facing that great crowd of inquiring people, unquestionably among them many of the rulers. The quick obedience to the Spirit and the enunciation of the truth as that truth dawned upon him, in answer to that inquiry; that is the first spiritual factor —his obedience to the Spirit in the witness he gave. Jesus had said, "Tarry in the city, until ye be clothed with power from on high," until you have received the Spirit, and then you shall be My witnesses. I think you will agree with me that, at this point, Peter was very conscious that he was speaking in actual fellowship with that Spirit. A little later on you will find he said so. In the fifth chapter, when they were arrested, and the Sanhedrin said to him, How dare you go on talking about this Jesus when we told you not to, Peter replied, "We must obey God rather than men," and then he added this significant thing, "And we are witnesses of these things; and so is the Holy Spirit, whom God hath given to them that obey him." And I think that here, at Pentecost, was his first consciousness. He was conscious of the Spirit, he was obedient to the Spirit, and all the wonder of that discourse is found, as to its reason, in that fact—a man speaking in obedience to that indwelling Spirit.

You will also notice that the Spirit has produced in Peter a new courage born of absolute conviction. Go through the sermon at your leisure, wonderful in its brevity when we consider all that is in it, as we go from stage to stage. You cannot find phrases such as, "it is reasonable to suppose," "in all probability," "so far as I can see," and "it seems to me." You do not find any of these, not a single one. Everything is—and don't be afraid of the word—dogmatic, definite, and authoritative. It is the language, not of a speculator, but of a confessor. It is not even the language of a soul trying to discover something. It is the language of a man to whom something has been revealed, and who can do none other than speak. He is convicted of the truth of the thing. And then, the clearness of the statement shows how this man had been given the illumination of the Spirit.

What is the next thing? Victory. That great crowd of believing souls had victory by the Spirit. For as Peter preached, he did not convince the crowd by his eloquence or his statement. The Spirit brought that conviction, but the Spirit needed that instrument to declare the truth. Do you see the wonderful cooperation that is revealed between the Spirit and the messenger of God who preaches? No man can bring conviction to men, even of the Deity of Christ, by his own argument.

Have you ever pulled yourself up seriously in front of this fact? In the sixteenth chapter of Matthew you have the account of how our Lord first spoke to His disciples about the Cross, and about the Church. Every student of the New Testament recognizes that, at Caesarea Philippi, when Peter made the great confession, there was a crisis. Everything up to that point had moved along certain lines. When that confession was made there was a change. Once that confession was made, our Lord began a new method. I do not mean to say that He had abandoned the old, or that it had failed. But the moment that confession was made, our Lord began to say things to His disciples that He had never said before. I am only dealing with the word of Scripture, not with any system of theology.

I do not stand for any school of theology. I simply stand for my Bible, and I want to be corrected by *it* when I am wrong.

Now you will find that directly Peter had made his confession, our Lord told His disciples three things he had never told them before. What were they? He told them He was going to build a Church. He had never referred to the Church until that moment. He told them He was going to the Cross. He had never explicitly told them about the Cross until then. He told them that the Son of God would come again in His glory. He had never told them that until then. He did not say whether His second coming would be "pre" or "post," and do not dissipate your own mental and spiritual power by wanting to argue round that. Of course, if a man says He is never coming again—well, that is something else; but *He* said He was coming. Three great secrets: the Church, the Cross, and the Coming. Never until Peter's confession at Caesarea Philippi had Jesus mentioned any of them. But when Peter said, "Thou art the Christ, the Son of the living God" immediately our Lord said, "Blessed art thou, Simon Bar-Jonah: for flesh and blood hath not revealed it unto thee, but My Father Who is in heaven. And I also say unto thee, that thou art Peter, and upon this rock I will build My Church; and the gates of Hades shall not prevail against it. I will give unto thee the keys of the kingdom of heaven: and whatsoever thou shalt bind on earth shall be bound in heaven; and whatsoever thou shalt loose on earth shall be loosed in heaven." (Now I have got to the place where I want to be.) *"Then charged he the disciples that they should tell no man that He was the Christ."* [6] I've been a long time getting there, have I not?"

Have you ever stopped to ask yourself what that means? Let me be frank with you. For years that thing baffled me. It always seemed to me as though Jesus would have said, This is what I have been waiting for. Men say I am Elijah, or John, or

Jeremiah, or one of the prophets. What do you say? "Thou art the Christ. . . ." Now it seems as though He should have said, Go and tell other men that. That is your business. But He did not say anything of the sort. He said, Do *not* tell anybody that. For years I could not understand it. You ask, "Do you now?" I think I do. I think it was because I am slow on the uptake that I never understood it before.

Look at it again. Peter said, "Thou art the Christ, the Son of the living God." Now listen to Jesus, "Blessed art thou, Simon Bar-Jonah; for flesh and blood hath not revealed it unto thee." That is merely a Hebrew idiom which means, No man told you that; that is something which cannot be proved by one man to another; that has come by Divine revelation. By what I am, you have learned the truth about Me, and My Father has revealed the truth about Me through Me. Now, do not go and tell men that.

He means, You cannot prove I am the Christ to any man. What were they to do? You go and bring men to Me; do not try to prove I am this, that, or the other. Get them to Me, and when they get to Me they will find out Who I am.

I do not intend to drive anybody else to that view, but that is where I stand. I am not to be out arguing about Jesus Christ. If I can get men to Him, really to Him, past the theologians, past the schoolmen, past the discussions of the philosophers; if I can get men to Him as He is here in these four Gospel narratives, which is God's method of preserving Him for our understanding—they will presently be saying with Thomas, "My Lord and my God." [7] The demonstration must be of the Spirit, but the Spirit needs the human instrument to declare the truth.

It is a great thing, my brother preacher,—and you know it as well as I do—to feel, when you are preaching Jesus, that there is Another at work in the hearts of the men and women you are talking to. He needs *you*. The Holy Spirit cannot do

His work apart from you. He needs you to tell that truth; but you also need Him if the thing you are telling is to be the power of God unto salvation. And you have, in Peter, the perfect cooperation of a man filled with the Spirit, telling the truth in obedience to the Spirit, with splendid clarity and absolute conviction. And because the Spirit was also on that crowd of listening people—for He had been poured upon all flesh—the conviction was that of sin, and righteousness, and judgment. For a man in cooperation with the Holy Spirit, the victory was won. That is the secret of the great result that followed.

Now, very generally, consider a reference to the matter of the sermon. First of all, notice that Peter went back to the Old Testament Scriptures. The choice of Joel is very interesting as I think we will come to see. Joel is one of the prophets that you must date either very early or very late. Many of the prophecies tell you when they were spoken. Isaiah does, Hosea does, but Joel does not. Joel has no date, and study will show it to be one of the earliest or one of the latest. Peter chose Joel, and he chose it because, in that prophecy as in no other, the prediction is given of the very things that were happening before their eyes.

Then he took the things of Jesus. Did you ever notice the wonderful sequence? First, Jesus, a Man, approved by miracles and wonders and signs. A Man, the perfect Man. The crucified, "Him, being delivered up by the determinate counsel and foreknowledge of God, ye by the hand of lawless men did crucify and slay." The risen Man, "God raised up, having loosed the pangs of death: because it was not possible that He should be holden of it." Then he goes aside to a psalm,[8] and quotes it to prove the accuracy of what he said. Do you see the Man? Jesus, a Man approved of God. Jesus, a Man crucified. Jesus, a Man raised, Jesus, a Man exalted to God's right hand, Jesus, a Man receiving a gift from the Father, Jesus, the Man,

pouring out the Holy Spirit—"He hath poured forth *this.*"
The personality of our Lord is introduced as Jesus of Nazareth; whatever that means in the first sentence, it means in the
very last. It is the same Person.

Then comes the great proclamation, that this same Jesus is
"Lord and Christ." So much for a general survey of the discourse, the physical, the mental, and the spiritual.

What were the results? To these we will come again; I just
name them now. Immediately, there was conviction and inquiry. They were convinced; "they were pricked in their
heart, and said unto Peter and the rest of the apostles, Brethren, what shall we do?" That was a new inquiry. The first was,
What does this mean? The second was, What must we do?
Then came instruction and exhortation. Peter told them exactly what to do, and exhorted them to do it forthwith. What
next? Obedience. They did what he told them to do. And then
addition: Were they added to the Church? It does not say so in
the text. "The Lord added. . . ." They were added *to the
Lord,* and so, of course, to the Church. That was the immediate result of that preaching: conviction, instruction, exhortation, obedience, and addition; or the growth of the Church.

The continuous results? They were all together at the end.
New ordinances were being observed: "They continued stedfastly in the apostles' teaching and fellowship, in the breaking
of bread and the prayers." It was a new way of life. Fear came
upon all, and many signs and wonders were wrought. No
man said "that aught of the things which he possessed was his
own; but they had all things common." A new experience of
life is described: They stayed "with one accord in the temple,
and breaking bread at home, they took their food with gladness and singleness of heart, praising God, and having favor
with all the people." And once again growth, "The Lord
added to them. . . ."

Such, in broad outline, is what remains of our chapter. We

close this study as we did the last, by noting the applications which are of permanent importance. First as to the Christian message. What is the Christian message? It is wholly a proclamation of what God has to say to man. The written Word— Peter went back to Joel. The living Word—he preached Jesus. Peter was the instrument through whom God proclaimed to men what He had to say. That is Christian preaching.

Then I note from the story that Christian preaching deals with the spiritual, and produces spiritual results which affect all of the life. The Christian preacher never begins with conditions. He begins with causes. His message is to the causes that underlie conditions, and through dealing with causes he reaches conditions. The Christian preacher is not primarily concerned with the suburbs but with the center; and when he delivers his message to the central things, all the suburbs are going to feel the effect of it—all the surroundings.

As a preacher I study this chapter again and again, perhaps none more often, and I feel that there is this revelation also: The Christian messenger must be a man who knows by experience as well as by theory. The Christian preacher must be, if he is to be really successful, a man who knows what it is to be filled with the Spirit. And the Christian preacher must have wisdom. That is another fine art of the Holy Spirit. When a man tells me he is filled with the Spirit, and is always making blundering mistakes in his dealings with men, I question whether he knows what it is to be filled with the Spirit. "He that is wise winneth souls." [9] That does not mean that you are a wise man if you win souls. It means that it takes a wise man to do it. It takes wisdom from above; and one thing the Holy Spirit gives to a man is common sense; or, if you like, tact.

There is a story of one of the great old presidents of a Methodist seminary, who used to address the freshmen students thus: "Now, gentlemen, three things are necessary in the work of God. You must have gifts, you must have grace, and you must have gumption." That is an old-fashioned word, but you know what it means. And he used to go on and say, "Gifts the Lord has bestowed upon you; grace He can administer to you in the process of your training, and we can help you; but if you have not gumption, neither God nor man can give it to you." I doubt if he was right on that point. In that last little twist of the statement I think he broke down. I think that if a man yields to the Spirit, He will give him gumption, and sanctified common sense that does not antagonize men by the first approach, but feels its way, and begins just where they are. Remember Paul in Athens. Not only did he quote from their poets, not only did he fasten upon one of their altars, but he began his address by saying, *not* "I perceive ye are very superstitious," but "I perceive that ye are very religious." [10] So they were. All idolatry is a demonstration of man's capacity for God. When Paul began, he did not antagonize. Neither did Peter, but before he was through he said things that must have made them quake. There was the art of the Holy Spirit in that message. May you and I learn better how to present our witness from this chapter.

CHAPTER 5

ACTS 2:14-21

We pass now to the first movement of Peter's message. We will stay there with the backward look; then we shall be ready to begin an examination of the second movement which begins at verse twenty-two. From there to the end of the chapter we have the first statement of Christian truth concerning Jesus from the lips of this prophet-apostle-evangelist, speaking in the power of the outpoured Spirit. And because that in some senses, is a matter of greatest value and interest and importance, we shall take three studies with it. Then, for the last two, we shall consider the results of this preaching, ending with a study that summarizes once again the spiritual value of what we have tried to do.

Now we begin at the fourteenth verse and go to the twenty-first. Peter is answering an inquiry, and does so by telling his listeners that the things they were seeing had been foretold in their own prophetic literature: *"This* is *that* which hath been spoken through the prophet Joel."* He took it for granted that they knew the prophecy of Joel, and said that the things they were looking at were the things that Joel foretold.

This is Peter's answer to the inquiry of the amazed, perplexed and critical multitude. You note that some of them had said mockingly that these people were drunk. It is always a temptation, when people are puzzled and cannot understand a thing, to mock at it. If a thing amazes you, it is not wrong to be amazed. If a thing perplexes you, it is not wrong to be perplexed. If you want to know about it, it is not wrong to ask questions. But you are always sure to be wrong when you laugh at the thing you do not understand. And in their mockery they said, "They are filled with new wine." In their mockery they came very near the truth, and as I said before, they were about as far from the truth as heaven is from hell. That paradox we will explore later.

Now, when Peter began to speak, he answered that criticism quite courteously. He said, "These are not drunken as ye suppose." In effect, You think these men are drunk; I am not surprised that you think so. It does look like it. But they are not drunken *in the way you mean,* "but *this* is *that.* . . ." Now let me leave that statement of being near, and yet as far apart as heaven is from hell, until later on. Let me quote again the words of Paul, so that you may keep them in the back of your mind: "Be not drunken with wine . . . but be filled with the Spirit." [1] The philosophy of that word of Paul is right at the back of this, and we will get to it by and by.

Now we proceed. Recognizing their right to inquire, and taking advantage of the opportunity it afforded him, Peter flung these men back to the prophecy with which they were, or ought to have been, familiar. The similarity between the manifestation which had aroused them and the things predicted by their prophet was so marked that he had a great starting point in answering their inquiry.

Please notice—and I do not desire to lay undue emphasis upon it, but I do not believe that any of the small things in Bible study are unimportant—that he addressed these men as, "Ye men of Judaea." The principal emphasis is there, though others were also included. Go back to verse five and you find "dwelling at Jerusalem Jews, devout men, from every nation under heaven." At verse twenty-two, when he began to talk about Jesus, he said, "Ye men of Israel, hear these words."

You do not need me to tell you that every Jew is a Hebrew, but every Hebrew is not a Jew. Nowadays we call them all Jews. We are not warranted in that at all. The Jews belong to Jewry; that is, to the kingdom of Judah, and in the kingdom of Judah you have the tribes of Judah and Benjamin. Strictly speaking, "Jews" belong only to those two tribes. Now, there are ten other tribes, also Hebrews but not Jews. Someone says, Well, those tribes are lost. But it is well for us to remember that when they returned from captivity under Ezra, Zerubbabel, and Nehemiah, it was not only Jews who came back. There were members of the other tribes who came back too. Not many, but there were some. In the time of our Lord all that dwelt in Judaea were not pure Jews. Members of some of the other tribes were there also.

I do not believe that when Peter said, in verse twenty-two, "Ye men of Israel," he was thinking only of the northern kingdom. He was using the name of the whole nation before its disruption. He was calling to *all* Hebrews, whether Judaeans or the others.

Of course you know, beloved, that nobody can read his Old Testament intelligently if he forgets that rupture of the kingdom after the death of Solomon, when the nation was divided into the northern kingdom of Israel and the southern kingdom of Judah. The northern kingdom was carried away into captivity a hundred years before the southern kingdom suffered the same fate; when they returned, the majority were of the tribe of Judah, but there were with them members of other tribes also. Peter had a purpose in addressing first the men of Judaea. He did not exclude the rest, but his first message was addressed especially to the men of Judaea.

Now, Joel's prophecy was addressed specifically to Judah, not to the northern kingdom. Three times he refers to Israel, but mainly to Judah. So that Peter is quoting from one who was a prophet to Judah, and the majority of his listeners were of Judah and Judaea. But, you say, does it matter? Only incidently, except that we are studying now. I am not preaching or lecturing; and I want you to see that if you watch your Bible carefully you will see that there is a reason, a system, and a definite orderliness in all this. These things are not haphazard. Very well, what he did was to go back to a prophecy whose message was distinctly to Judah, and he quoted that prophecy. Having said to them *"This* is *that,"* he quoted *"that"* to explain "this." So that if anyone wants a ready-made sermon, here you have it with its divisions. The text, "This is that." First, "this;" secondly, "that;" thirdly, the relation between "this" and "that." That is a good homiletic outline. So let us go back with Peter to "that" which was written by the prophet Joel.

I suggested that you should read the prophecy of Joel in preparation. It is very brief; only three chapters. There ought to be four. Some clever arrangers thought they could improve on the Hebrew divisions. I will tell you at once what I mean.

In the Hebrew Bible this part that Peter quotes is a chapter all by itself. Now look at the prophecy and you will see, at the second chapter, verse twenty-eight, the commencement of Peter's quotation: "And it shall come to pass afterward, that I will pour out My Spirit upon all flesh" and so on, until he came to the end of the second chapter (in the prophecy) which is really the third chapter in the Hebrew Bible. So that Peter was quoting a whole, complete chapter from the Hebrew Bible. I have no doubt that he quoted from the Septuagint, the Greek version which was the version our Lord and the apostles used.

The prophecy of Joel is full of interest. As I intimated in our last study, it has no date. You can only estimate the date by inference from its content. In comparison, the prophecy just before this, the prophecy of Hosea, is definitely dated:

> The word of Jehovah that came unto Hosea the son of Beeri, in the days of Uzziah, Jotham, Ahaz, and Hezekiah, kings of Judah, and in the days of Jeroboam the son of Joash, king of Israel.

You see you have the two kingdoms mentioned there, and if you want to follow up that research you will see that Hosea was exercising his ministry at exactly the same time as Isaiah. Isaiah opens with the declaration that his prophetic ministry was exercised in the days of Uzziah, Jotham, Ahaz and Hezekiah—at the time Hosea's was.

There is a great deal being written and said about modern attempts to date these prophecies. I only ask you to trust the dates *inside* the prophecies themselves, and do not allow anybody to change them for you. I am not saying this without consideration, but upon the basis of the conclusions of profound scholarship. How many profound scholars of the Hebrew Bible are there today, who can be reckoned as experts? You can count them on the fingers of your hand. There was one in this country, and he was not to be matched on the Continent or anywhere. I am referring to Robert Dick Wilson of Princeton Theological Seminary (later of Westminster Theological Seminary). He knew more about the Hebrew language than anyone living. He had been forty-five years getting ready for the work he accomplished and when he sat down to work he had an intimate knowledge of at least forty languages bearing upon the Bible. I have not had time for that; but believe me when I say, do not change your dates.

There is nothing in Joel to date his prophecy. There is no reference to kings that will help you. You will not find his father, Pethuel, anywhere else, or Joel anywhere else. Very well, the next thing the student does is to notice the things this man does, or does not say—local color. This process proves that Joel was either one of the earliest of the prophets or one of the latest. For instance, he makes no reference to the Assyrians, or the Chaldeans. That puts the prophecy either before the Assyrian and Chaldean invasions, or after. And, as I have said, he makes no reference whatever to kings. Now, that is a striking fact. It does not mean there were no kings, but that he exercised his ministry in some period when the kings, because of their failure, were overshadowed by the prophets. He refers to priests and to rulers. That does not help much, but it does put him outside certain periods. Again, he does not refer to idolatry or a moral corruption of the people—not all the way through his prophecy. He does not pour scorn on the sacrifices, as some of them did. Oh, yes, he does lament the locust plague that has made it impossible for the sacrifices to be brought to the temple; and all the way through, the temple is in existence. These things give you suggestive background, but do not enable you to be dogmatic about the dating. It does exclude the period from Ahaz to Hezekiah. You will find things here which are found in other prophecies. You say, that must prove that Joel was early. Not at all. Perhaps he was quoting from them. Someone says, That means Joel was late. Not at all. Perhaps they were quoting from him. That dismisses the background. You cannot place him definitely.

But no prophet is clearer in his message or intention, and you can discover local conditions, even though you may not be able to date historically the time of those conditions.

First, he interpreted to the nation a calamity that had overtaken them in the visit of a locust plague which had swept the whole land bare of harvest and of verdure. Once, years ago in a southern state, there had been just such a plague, and I traveled over that area just after it had happened. Locusts had swept over a piece of land about twenty miles wide, and forty miles in length, and they had not left a blade of grass, or a leaf on a tree. In like manner, in the prophecy, the locust plague had taken everything, and the people were impoverished by it. Then the prophet comes, and his first message has to do with this calamity: "Hear this, ye old men, and give ear, all ye inhabitants of the land. . . ." That is verse two. Verse five: "Awake, ye drunkards, and weep. . . ." Verse eight: "Lament. . . ." and so on.

What is this man doing? He is declaring to the nation that the thing they were looking upon as mere calamity, was an act of God in judgment. He told them that the locust plague was "the day of the Lord"—that God had been acting. They were doing just what we do today; lamenting over a calamity, just as we do a war, and trying to account for it within the boundaries of human policies and diplomacies; mourning over the sorrow of it, and missing the great moral and spiritual lesson that the Lord reigneth. In the first message, after describing the devastation caused by the plague, he says, "Alas for the day! for the day of Jehovah is at hand." That does not mean it was coming. It was there. He said, You are living in the day of the Lord *now*. This is the act of God.

Now, in chapter two of the prophecy, verses one through twenty-seven (the second chapter in the Hebrew Bible), there are two divisions. Verse one: "Blow ye the trumpet in Zion, and sound an alarm. . . ." Verse fifteen: "Blow the trumpet in Zion, sanctify a fast. . . ." There are two movements in this second message. He is telling them that they are in danger. They are in danger of an invasion. He is dealing with a political situation, and these old Hebrew prophets often did that.

It is a great temptation to stay there. When a man tells me that as a preacher he has nothing to do with politics, I must tell him that he does not understand the genius of the Christian faith. If he means he has no part in party politics, I agree with him. Whenever the Christian Church has been captured by any party, she has been paralyzed. But it is the duty of the Christian preacher and the Church to dictate terms of righteousness to all political parties, to kings and emperors and governors, to parliaments and municipalities. If your church has nothing to say to the civic authorities about the moral conditions of your city, you are failing in your duty. Oh, yes, you say, but we are all going to be taken out of this by and by. Blessed be God, that is my hope too, but I differ entirely from any man who holds the view that, because of this hope, he has no moral responsibility for the city in which he lives. The Church of God is called upon to hold the keys of the Kingdom; the keys of the Kingdom are the insignia of the scribe—moral interpretation.

Well, that is another aside. These old prophets dealt with such situations, and Joel saw that the nation was in positive danger from an invading army. And he employed what they had actually experienced, a locust plague, to illustrate the more terrible thing that was at hand, the invading army. "Blow ye the trumpet in Zion, and sound an alarm." What does he want to sound an alarm for? Seeing the devastation of the plague, he said to the people, This is the day of the Lord! God is abroad and you have not recognized that. God is governing. Then he climbed to a height and looked ahead, seeing an invasion imminent and the peril of it. "Blow the trumpet in Zion, sanctify a fast!" The thing that threatens you is by the act and government of God. It is the day of the Lord! The day of the Lord! The day of the Lord!

You find this all through your Bible, for the prophets all copy from him and quote from him. Though I have not said it before, my own conviction is that he is the earliest of the prophets. He says, That locust plague is the day of the Lord. You are living in the midst of it. That army that threatens to invade you is the day of the Lord. The day of the Lord is here, it is imminent, it is close at hand. God is acting. There are the first two movements of the prophecy.

What then? "And it shall come to pass afterward, that I will pour out My Spirit upon all flesh. . . ." *Afterward.* Now, there is the advantage of retaining the Hebrew division and making this an entirely new chapter. *After* the locust plague; *after* the terrors of an invading army which will come unless you repent; *after* that, "I will pour out My Spirit."

Now in *your* thinking, where have you put the dating of Joel? Even if you are one of those who put him very late among the prophets, you still have at least three hundred years between the time he uttered his prophecy and this day of Pentecost when Peter was quoting him. So that between the end of his first message and the thing he is now saying, at least three hundred years have passed. Here is a great illustration of the prophetic outlook. Here is this Hebrew prophet, borne along by the Spirit; he saw the immediate, and interpreted it; he saw the invading army, and interpreted it as "the day of the Lord." And then, suddenly, looking down the vista of the years and the centuries, he saw somewhere, away in the distance, the fulfillment of this prediction: "It shall come to pass . . . that I will pour out My Spirit upon all flesh." That is his third prophecy.

Peter told that multitude in Jerusalem that they had seen that prediction of three or four hundred years before, fulfilled before their eyes. *"This* is *that."*

What did Joel see?

And it shall come to pass afterward, that I will pour out My Spirit upon all flesh; and your sons and your daughters shall prophesy, your old men shall dream dreams, your young men shall see visions; and also upon the servants and upon the handmaidens in those days will I pour out My Spirit.

My brothers and sisters, as Bible students can you possibly put yourselves back in time, not to the day of Pentecost, but those hundreds of years before it, and listen to this message as though you had been among those who heard it for the first time? Do you notice how it cuts clean across all the prejudices of the Jewish people? Here is a prophet saying things that trampled all those prejudices underfoot. "I will pour out My Spirit upon all flesh," not merely upon Israel, not merely upon God's ancient people, but upon *all flesh.* "And your sons and your daughters shall prophesy." You know the prejudices of the Hebrew people against the idea of a woman prophesying, in spite of the history of Deborah. In the time of Christ the strict Pharisee had a prayer of thanksgiving that fell from his lips every day; and I have no doubt that Saul of Tarsus prayed it, "O God, I thank Thee that I am not a Gentile, that I am not a slave, that I am not a woman." Paul must have had this in mind when he said that, in Christ, there cannot be Jew or Greek, bond or free, male or female. He was contradicting the false conception that had characterized the life of the Pharisees.

Yea and on My servants and on My handmaidens in those days will I pour forth of My Spirit; and they shall prophesy.[2]

Joel looked on and saw a day when that very thing was going to happen.

Now follow him carefully, please:

And I will show wonders in the heavens and in the earth: blood, and fire, and pillars of smoke. The sun shall be turned into darkness, and the moon into blood, before the great and terrible day of Jehovah cometh.[3]

96

The day of the Lord still. The locust plague, he said, is the day of the Lord. It is God Who is acting. Imminent invasion— that is the day of the Lord. God is governing. And then, looking far along, he speaks of "the great and terrible day of the Lord." Yes, but before that day comes, he says, there is going to be this strange and wonderful period when the Spirit is to be poured out upon all flesh; when sons and daughters shall prophesy; when the bondslaves, men and women, shall possess this great Spirit-filled power. And *then,* he says—mind, it is a straight line of continuity—God will show these wonders, blood, fire, vapor of smoke, the sun turned into darkness and the moon into blood, *before* the great and terrible day of the Lord comes. Beyond the period of the outpoured Spirit, Joel saw this great and terrible day of the Lord. He says that before that day comes there will be these signs in the heavens, and he says, "Whosoever shall call on the name of Jehovah shall be delivered." [4] From what? From that great and terrible day of the Lord. And yet it is a day of deliverance, "for in Mount Zion and in Jerusalem there shall be those that escape, as Jehovah hath said, and among the remnant those whom Jehovah doth call." [5] It is a clear perspective of coming events as Joel saw them.

In the next chapter he begins, "For, behold, in those days, and in that time, when I shall bring back the captivity of Judah and Jerusalem, I will gather all nations. . . ." [6] In that time, still far ahead, the great and terrible day would result in the restoration of Jacob and the building of Jerusalem. And between these periods he saw a gap, an unmeasured span of time, that he did not call the day of the Lord, but the day of the outpoured Spirit. It is historic, prophetic presentation. Just as you might stand at the end of a street where the lights are not at mathematical intervals. You cannot see the end of it, and no man can tell the distance between the fifteenth lamp and the sixteenth; so this is not a measured distance. You cannot make a calendar of this, and say it will begin here and end there; but the processional activity of God in human history is clearly marked, and right in the midst of it is this unmeasured period.

Now for a moment take the phrase, "the day of Pentecost" in the light of this prophetic interpretation. Historically, the phrase marks the commencement of the period that the prophet described. It was on a definite day that this thing began, the day of Pentecost, or the feast of weeks, as the Hebrews called it. But the day of Pentecost has another significance. It covers the characteristics of a period, an unmeasured period, and there is nothing in your Bible that will enable you to measure it; nothing, absolutely nothing that will give you any idea of how long that period is to last. It has lasted now more than nineteen hundred years. How many more? I have no idea, and you have not, and no one has; and the moment you and I begin trying by any means to find out the measurement of this period, we are violating one of the true principles of Bible study and research. It is the period which Joel predicted, and it moves toward the final movement of an established order. You and I are living in this day of Pentecost. This is the day of the Holy Spirit, when sons and daughters prophesy; when the Spirit is poured out upon the servants as well as their masters, the handmaidens as well as their mistresses. The day when, by the Spirit, old men dream dreams and young men see visions. The day is still proceeding, the darkness is ahead. But even that darkness will be the darkness that presages the dawn of God's day that never wanes, but remains eternal noon in His great victory.

Mark the expression again—the Spirit was *poured forth*. The Spirit of God is found active throughout your Bible, but something happened that day that had never happened before. You will find the Spirit of God at the very beginning of the Genesis record: "The Spirit of God brooded over the face of the chaos." Make your way through the Old Testament, and you will find the Spirit referred to as coming to men and then leaving them, sometimes coming briefly for some specific purpose. I am quoting the expression, "clothing Himself with a man," as He did in the case of Gideon; sometimes He is said to clothe a man with Himself. He came upon men to make them cunning workers in gold and silver for the work of the tabernacle. He came upon prophets; but there was no permanent residence of the Spirit of God in human souls until the day of Pentecost. *Then* He was poured forth, and poured forth to remain and abide in that holy vessel the Church, which that day was born, and has grown by the addition of all such as, believing on Jesus Christ, have received the new life.

Joel said that the Spirit should be poured out upon "all flesh." All flesh—not merely upon that company in the upper room. The Spirit came to begin a new ministry in the world on the basis of the work that our Lord had accomplished. That day, the Spirit came to fulfill a ministry in the world that He had never been able to do before.

Our Lord told his disciples:

It is expedient for you that I go away; for if I go not away, the Comforter (the Holy Spirit) will not come unto you; but if I go, I will send Him unto you. And He, when He is come, will convict the world in respect of sin, and of righteousness, and of judgment: of sin, because they believe not on Me; of righteousness, because I go to the Father, and ye behold Me no more; of judgment, because the prince of this world hath been judged.[7]

"He will convict the world," and the Spirit was poured out, not only to fill the believer, but to rest upon humanity everywhere. When next you preach, my friend, my brother in the ministry, do not forget that the Spirit is working with the people who hear. He is there to convict. This new movement results from the mighty work which has been accomplished by the Son of God. "In the beginning was the Word, and the Word was with God, and the Word was God. . . . And the Word became flesh." [8] That means identification with humanity, and the Spirit was poured upon all flesh because of what had been done by the Word made flesh.

With what result? Prophesying. Now, prophecy is not only prediction. Prediction is prophesy, but only one small phase of it. The old prophets never predicted coming events to satisfy the curiosity, even of the godly. There was always a moral intention in prophecy. Prophecy is the forthtelling of the will of God. "Your sons and your daughters shall prophesy."

Remember the day when some people went to Moses, very much troubled because some others were exercising gifts, but not in regular orders? And there came from Moses' heart a great cry: "Would God that all the Lord's people were prophets!" [9] When the Spirit came, that is what happened. He came to make all people of God prophets, witnesses; not necessarily preachers, but men and women who speak the Word of God to others. Your sons and your daughters, your servants and handmaidens, bond and free, male and female, Jew and Gentile. All caste divisions swept away, and the empowerment of humanity would become the mouthpiece of the Word of God.

Another wonderful expression: "Your old men shall dream dreams, and your young men shall see visions." Dreams you have when you are resting; old men shall dream dreams. Visions come when you are wide awake; your young men shall see visions. Dreams are mostly concerned with past experiences. Visions are anticipatory. I am getting more interested in dreams than I used to be. "Your old men shall dream dreams, your young men shall see visions." There it is left in its poetic beauty.

We close this study by going back to its beginning. *"This* is *that.* . . ." These men are not drunken as ye suppose. You are near the truth, but you are as far off as heaven is from hell. Why did Paul say, "Be not drunk with wine . . . but be filled with the Spirit"? [10] Why did he put these two statements together? Because they are close together. Why does a man get drunk? No man living ever drank alcohol in any form in order presently to lie incapable in the gutter. There is only one reason. A man drinks, and for the moment he is conscious of an uplift. He is lifted above the drab and the commonplace. I know what you are saying. The reaction lets him down deeper than the place from which he rose. But the power of the alcohol within him lifted him. He was the politician who could have dismissed all politicians; he was a king then; he was lifted. Oh, the tragedy of it! I overheard two men talking not long ago. They were talking about soft drinks, and at last one said to the other, "Poor stuff, George." And the other said, "Yes, there's no kick in it." What do you mean by "kick"? It is a lift! A man takes drink because it lifts him. "Be not drunken with wine," says Paul; do not get that kind of lift "wherein is riot" that lets you down, "but be filled with the Spirit" and get the lift that never lets you down; the elevation of life that makes you superior to circumstance and the commonplace. Look, said the mocking crowd, these people are drunk! No, says Peter, they are not drunk in the way you mean. This is what I mean when I say that they were near the truth, yet as far off as heaven is from hell. These men were filled with the Holy Spirit.

There is a question that comes to me, rather an amazing question, perhaps; but I will put it to you. Did anybody ever think you were drunk because of your Christianity? I know exactly what you are saying: No, thank God! Well now, that is what is the matter with the Christian church. We have lost our passion. We have lost our capacity for tears and laughter and joy. There is so little light in our eyes! So halfhearted are our songs! We even sing a hymn that says we cannot sing!

> Hosannas languish on our tongues,
> And our devotion dies.

And that describes most of the singing I hear in the churches! It is nothing to boast about. I am not asking for anything in the nature of excitement. Painted fires do not burn. But when the Spirit fills the Church, the Church is on fire, and the city will ask, What does this mean?

CHAPTER • 6

ACTS 2:22-24

In the rest of Peter's discourse, which occupies verses twenty-two to thirty-six, he starts in simple yet sublime and exhaustive sentences to trace the process culminating in Pentecost in regard to Jesus.

We begin at verse twenty-two:

> Jesus of Nazareth, a Man approved of God unto you by mighty works and wonders and signs which God did by Him in the midst of you, even as ye yourselves know; Him, being delivered up by the determinate counsel and foreknowledge of God, ye by the hand of lawless men did crucify and slay: Whom God raised up, having loosed the pangs of death: because it was not possible that He should be holden of it.

He has reached the point of resurrection, and he declares the reason for that great affirmation of conviction: "It was impossible that He should be holden of it," that is, of death. Now notice that verses twenty-five to thirty-two form a parenthesis dealing with the resurrection. For the moment let us leave it out and follow the sequence at verse thirty-three. Read verse twenty-four, and skip from there to verse thirty-three, for that is a sequence of statement. I do not mean that the parenthesis is unimportant. It is so important that we will do nothing in our next study but examine it. It is as important and illuminative and interpretive as the passage we are looking at here. But I want you to get the sequence.

> . . . Whom God raised up, having loosed the pangs of death: because it was not possible that He should be holden of it. . . . Being therefore by the right hand of God exalted, and having received of the Father the promise of the Holy Spirit, He hath poured forth this, which ye see and hear.

Then follows another parenthesis, "For David ascended not into the heavens: but he saith himself. . . ." and so on. Then comes the proclamation, the final thing in his address:

> Let all the house of Israel therefore know assuredly, that God hath made him both Lord and Christ, this Jesus Whom ye crucified.

There is the whole address. It opens with "Jesus of Nazareth." It ends with "this Jesus whom ye crucified," and in the process of it, the Apostle has accounted for the things they were looking at with such amazement; he associates them with Jesus of Nazareth and declares how these things have come to pass through Him.

Still looking at the general movement, leaving out the parenthesis that refers to resurrection, you will notice a sequence of facts declared. First, "Jesus of Nazareth." Now do not read, "Jesus of Nazareth a man", because those two words, "a man" belong to something else that is coming. "Jesus of Nazareth," that is the first fact; a Person is named.

The next fact, "a man approved of God unto you." "*Unto*

you." What does that mean? It is not a declaration of Divine approbation, but it is a declaration of the Divine demonstration of approbation, "approved *unto you*." How? "By mighty works and wonders and signs which God did by Him in the midst of you, even as ye yourselves know." There is the second fact. First, we have the Person of Jesus of Nazareth; secondly, we have the perfection of that Person as demonstrated by the mighty works and wonders and signs; that is, the perfection of His humanity is demonstrated by the miracles.

Now notice the next thing. "Him, being delivered up by the determinate counsel and foreknowledge of God, ye by the hand of lawless men did crucify and slay." There is your third fact—that Person in death.

"Whom God raised up, having loosed the pangs of death: because it was not possible that He should be holden of it." There is your fourth fact—resurrection.

"Being therefore by the right hand of God exalted"—ascension. Remember, it is Jesus of Nazareth all the time; and when you are thinking this through, do not lose sight of Him now. Do not imagine that the Man of Nazareth has been dissipated into thin air; it is the same Person, "being by the right hand of God exalted." That is your fifth fact.

What next? "Having received of the Father the promise of the Holy Spirit . . ." The reception of the Spirit by the exalted Man in Glory.

What is the last fact? "He hath poured forth *this*." Pentecost, the result of a process.

To my young friends I say, Get this passage and ponder it long and carefully. Remember, this is the first statement of truth concerning Jesus Christ from the lips of a man filled with the Holy Spirit. There are many things you will not find here. There is nothing in this first sermon about His intercessory work as Priest. There is not a word about His coming again. There is nothing about His ultimate governing work. It is simply a description of the process that culminated in Pentecost.

In Peter's next discourse over in the third chapter, (and I beg you to keep your New Testament entire; do not get a mutilated copy of it), he talks about this Christ Who is coming to act. But here on the day of Pentecost, in order to account for the phenomenon of the Church—I do not like the word phenomenon here—the mystery of the Church—that is Scriptural; in order to account for that to the inquiring city, Peter links prophecy with Jesus, and shows the steps which led to it: His Person, His perfection, His death, His resurrection, His ascension and exaltation, His reception of and His pouring out of the Spirit—God's dealing with humanity through the risen and exalted Man, Jesus.

The central fact here, and the one concerning which Peter turned aside in that wonderful parenthesis, is resurrection. These are the seven facts: three preceding the resurrection, then the resurrection, then three following—His exaltation, His reception of the Spirit, and His pouring out of that Spirit.

Let us look quite briefly, but reverently, at the first movement in Peter's sermon: the Person, His perfection and His passion. Notice how he began: "Jesus of Nazareth."

We are so familiar with this phrase that we are in danger of losing the significance of it. Peter, speaking to that crowd of people, named Him as He was known to them. That is how they spoke of Him, Who had walked about their cities and villages, through their highways and up and down their byways; into Whose eyes they had looked, Whose language was theirs, Whose hands had wrought many mighty works. And Peter names Him so. He does not give Him the title of Christ. He does not even call Him Lord. He begins with the fact of the human Jesus, "Jesus of Nazareth," the designation by which He was familiarly known.

106

According to these records it was Philip who first called Him that. He went to find Nathanael and said, "We have found Him, of Whom Moses in the law, and the prophets, wrote, Jesus of Nazareth." [1] Nathanael said, "Can any good thing come out of Nazareth?"

Do not misunderstand Nathanael. That was not contempt for Nazareth from the standpoint of a Judaean, for Nathanael was from Galilee. He would not have spoken disrespectfully of Nazareth for the reason that it was a town in Galilee. It has been said that he was using a proverb. I think it is the revelation of a fact too often lost sight of that Nazareth was, at that time, a seething hotbed of corruption. That fact lies behind all the account of the birth of Jesus. Philip called Him Jesus of Nazareth, and that is how people came to speak of Him. A demon-possessed man said, "What have we to do with Thee, Jesus Thou Nazarene?" [2] When He entered Judaea the Judaean miltitudes said, "Who is this?" and the Galileans accompanying Him answered, "This is the prophet, Jesus, from Nazareth of Galilee." [3] In the garden when the soldiers came seeking Him, He said, "Whom seek ye?" and they said, "Jesus of Nazareth." [4] That night in the outer court, when Peter was warming himself by the fire of the enemies of his Lord, the maid said to him, "Thou also wast with the Nazarene, even Jesus." [5] When Pilate wrote His title and put it on the cross, it read, "JESUS OF NAZARETH, THE KING OF THE JEWS." [6]

The interest and the wonder grows. The angel at the tomb said, "Be not amazed: ye seek Jesus, the Nazarene, Who hath been crucified: He is risen; He is not here." [7] And once more, as two friends were walking to Emmaus, this risen One joined them and they did not recognize Him. He asked, What are you talking about? Why are you sad? And they in astonishment said to Him, Are you a lodger in Jerusalem, and don't

107

you know the things that have been happening there? And He said, What things? And they said, "The things concerning Jesus the Nazarene." [8]

Well, that covers some of the ground. The point is that this is how He had come to be known.

"Jesus" as you know, is the Greek form of "Joshua," and there is tremendous significance in that. I suggest to you that when Jesus was born and so named, there were hundreds of boys bearing this name in Judaea and Galilee. He was given one of the most commonplace names of the times. "Joshua" was as common among the boys then as "John" is today. Does that sound strange to you? It is not at all. Why did so many parents name their boys Joshua? Two great figures of the Hebrew people had borne that name in the past. One was the high priest in the time of Zechariah.[9] And there had been another, the successor of Moses; and I think many boys were named after him. That boy was born in Egypt before the exodus. His parents called him Hoshea; I think that in that naming of a baby born in Egypt there was a sob and a sigh, and a ray of hope in the future. Hoshea means salvation. How did he become Joshua? Moses made that name for him when he knew that this young man was to be his successor. Moses called him Jehoshua.[10] That is as near as we can get to it. He took the Hebrew name which means salvation, and interwove with it parts of the great incommunicable Name of God that you and I call "Jehovah." The word, Jehovah, is a modern form of the word, because the Hebrew people never wrote the name, nor pronounced it. In the Hebrew Bible you find the four consonants, YHVH. When it stood for the name Yahweh, or Jehovah, it meant the Becoming One, the One who in grace bows and bends and stoops and becomes; for Yahweh is not a part of the verb "to be," but of the verb "to become." It was the great name by which God had made Himself known to His people in grace; not Elohim, which stood for His might and majesty, nor Adonai, which stood for His supremacy and Lordship, but Yahweh, which stood for what He becomes to His people. Moses took that word and the word "salvation" and named this young man Jehoshua, the salvation of Jehovah.

And when Jesus was to be born, the angel said to Joseph, "Thou shalt call His name JESUS (Joshua); for it is *He* that shall save his people from their sins." [11]

But in Nazareth I do not think they stopped to think about that. When they heard His name in Judaea I do not think they were remembering the history of the name or its profound significance. They did as people so often do—they linked Him up with His home town. Every Welshman understands this. Go to Wales and talk, for instance, about the man who wrote, "Guide me O Thou great Jehovah." If you say William Williams wrote it, no one knows what you mean. But say Williams of Wern wrote it, and everyone knows. They link the man with his town. Let us get down to the human level here, because that is where we begin. "Jesus of Nazareth." Someone they all knew. His name had passed into the common currency of human speech. Hundreds who had not seen Him knew Him by that phrase. His fame had gone out through all Syria, and from everywhere they crowded after Him.

Now Peter, in preaching, says, "Jesus of Nazareth." He has marked Him and defined Him by the use of the name and title that had become the common currency of reference to Him. Always keep in mind that this Person, Jesus of Nazareth, never passes from sight all the way through the discourse. It is the same Person doing mighty works; it is the same Person going to the Cross; it is the same Person coming out of the tomb, being exalted and receiving the Holy Spirit and pouring Him out. He is Jesus of Nazareth; He is God's Man as Luke portrays Him; He is the "second Man" and the "last Adam" as Paul describes Him.[12] *Not* the "second Adam."

That mistake is made in some of our hymns and devotional literature and theological books. Paul did not say so. Do you say, That is a little thing, it does not matter? But it *does* matter if you are careful in your thinking. The word "Adam" is used here as referring to the founder of a race. And Paul looked back and said, That man in the garden of Eden, he was the first Adam. Here is God's second Man and He is the last Adam. There will be no third. This One will fulfill the Divine ideal for humanity where the first failed. "Jesus of Nazareth." That is the first fact.

Let us particularly notice what Peter then said. "A Man approved of God unto you." The verb means "demonstrated *by* God *to* you." What is the demonstration? "Approved of God unto you by mighty works and wonders and signs." It is a very significant thing that, in the first address delivered in the power of the outpoured Spirit, Peter uses the three words in the New Testament record which you and I generally call miracles. That word "miracle" comes from the Latin tongue. Sometimes I wish that we had some other word. But here are the three New Testament words: miracles, wonders, and signs. The American Standard Version translates them as "mighty works and wonders and signs." But if you look at the marginal note (and you young folk, always keep your eye on the margin) you will see an alternative—"powers, wonders, and signs." "Powers" is the best word. "Mighty works" may help us, but "powers" is better. These are the things Jesus did, not describing three different sorts of acts, but describing anything you and I call the miraculous. Turning water into wine? Yes, if you like. Raising Lazarus from the dead? Yes, if you please. The Virgin Birth? Yes, if you so please. Anything you and I call the miraculous or supernatural; only when you use that word, you are talking about something that is above what you know in Nature. There is nothing supernatural to God. The supernatural is simply something that transcends our understanding. That is all. That is the meaning of miracle. A miracle is something that creates wonder—there is your second word. Your third word is signs. Take any one of them; it was a power. If you had seen Lazarus come out of the tomb you would have said, There is power. If you had seen water turned into wine, you would have said, There is power. You do not know what power operated in order to turn water into wine. You do not know what power operated in order to bring that dead man back to life.

"Signs" is the word John used to apply to all these things. What is the meaning of the word "sign" whenever you find it in the New Testament? A sign is something that proves that out of which it came, because it could have come out of nothing else. Let me use an illustration. In Canada they have a symbol, the maple leaf. It is not a sign in the New Testament sense of the word. Every sign is a symbol, but every symbol is not a sign. Why is not the maple leaf the sign of Canada? Because there are also maple trees in the United States. It does not prove Canada at all. If I were on the other side of the world, and saw in a book the picture of a maple leaf, I would not immediately think of Canada. A Canadian would, but I would not. I would say, I wonder if that picture is of a leaf in Canada or in the United States. Another illustration: How many of you have heraldic bearings in your family tree? They are symbols, not signs. But if they have your fingerprints on them anywhere, they are signs. They prove *you,* because no other fingerprints in the world are the same as yours. John says that these "works" were signs, demonstrating the one fact that Jesus of Nazareth was the Son of God.

Now look again at what Peter is saying: "A man approved of God unto you by powers and wonders and signs which He did in the midst of you." Is that right? Did I read that correctly? No. I read it wrong purposely in order that you might see how constantly we read carelessly. Let me read it again. "A man approved of God unto you by mighty works and wonders and signs which *God did by Him* in the midst of you, even as ye yourselves know." There you have one of the most remarkable statements in the New Testament about the miracles which Jesus wrought. Yes, in a certain sense He did perform them. But Peter, on the day of Pentecost, in the full intelligence that had come to Him through the Holy Spirit, does not put it so. He says, God did them by His Son. He was the instrument of a Divine activity. Whenever you read of a miracle it is an action of God, and was not wrought, even by the human Jesus apart from the fact that His humanity was the instrument of Divine action. That is fundamental. Let me put it startlingly. Jesus, in His human form, performed no miracles. You say, What do you mean by that? I mean what Peter said. God wrought the miracles through Jesus. They were miracles "which God did *by Him* in the midst of you." Consequently the miracles prove, not the Deity of our Lord, but His humanity—His perfect humanity. Oh, yes, His Deity is proved in other ways, and sublimely; but the miracles prove the absolute perfection of His manhood. Are you seeing why I emphasize it? "A *Man* approved of God. . . ." And the perfection of His humanity made Him the instrument through which God could do these things which you and I call miracles. Powers which create wonder; and signs of the perfection of His humanity, and of the Divine power operating through Him.

Now, if you challenge me at that point, it is good that you do so, lest any should say I am undervaluing the fact of the Deity of our Lord. Nothing of the kind. The proof lies in the other direction. Jesus of Nazareth is a Man of my humanity. This is the name and title by which everybody knew Him. And He was so much one with men that they saw no difference in His appearance. John the Baptist said, "There standeth One in the midst of you, Whom ye know not." [13] There was no halo round His brow, nothing that marked Him out from others. But Peter says God has approved Him "by mighty works and wonders and signs." All the powers that created your wonder were signs, a divine action demonstrated through an absolutely perfect human being. There are two facts in this great movement. First a Man, a Person, Jesus of Nazareth, verily human and near to me; and yet at the same time He is put away from me, separated from me in the absolute perfection of His humanity as distinguished from the imperfection and failure of mine. A Man, yes, approved of God, demonstrated by the signs He did. And there has been none other. Oh, but you say, these others worked miracles, too. How? Always in the name of Jesus Christ; and everything that happened after was done in the power of His life. Remember these two facts; the actuality of the Person, Jesus of Nazareth; and His perfection as demonstrated by those very powers and wonders and signs.

Passing on, Peter says, "Him . . ." notice how careful he is to keep your eyes on the same Person—"Him, being delivered up by the determinate counsel and foreknowledge of God, ye by the hand of lawless men did crucify and slay." This is the first reference to the Cross after Pentecost, and the man who makes it is Peter, the great representative disciple. Peter is speaking eight weeks after the Cross; the Cross was therefore foremost in their minds. But let us go back to six months before the Cross. Where do you find them? In the eighth chapter of Mark, or the sixteenth of Matthew, you find yourself at Caesarea Philippi at the hour in which Our Lord, having led His disciples away up there to the northeast, asked them what all His teaching and preaching and working of miracles amounted to. He said, "Who do men say that the Son of man is?" He had been among people for two and a half years, eighteen months in definite and intentional public propaganda. Now He says, "Who do men say that I am?" And they told Him, dear hearts, the best things they had heard about Him. I cannot help stressing that. They told Him the *best* things. "Some say Elijah, others John the Baptist, others Jeremiah, or one of the prophets." The answer came out of the kindness of their hearts. You say, What are you driving at? I mean this. They might have said to Him, Well, Lord, we do not care to mention it, but some of them say You have a devil. When a man says he does not care to tell you anything, and then tells you, he is a liar. He wanted to tell you! No, they told Him the best things. But He was not satisfied. Nothing they had told Him was sufficient. He said, "Who do *you* say that I am?" and Peter said, "Thou art the Christ, the Son of the living God."

Directly that confession was made, our Lord began to teach them about the Cross. "From that time began Jesus to show unto His disciples, that He must go unto Jerusalem, and suffer many things of the elders and chief priests and scribes, and be killed, and the third day be raised up." [14] He *began*. Now watch Peter. What did he say? God help you, not that! Spare Thyself, not that! And Jesus sternly rebuked him, "Get thee behind Me, Satan: thou art a stumbling-block unto Me: for thou mindest not the things of God, but the things of men."

Will you forgive me if I say I want you to sympathize with Peter? I know the Lord rebuked him, but I understand his attitude that day. The wrath of the Lord was not so much for what he had said as for not resting in the authority of his Master. What was Peter objecting to? If you had been following Jesus for two and a half years and heard Him reveal the great ideals of the Kingdom; if you had been enamored of those ideals, captured by them, how would you have felt if you had heard Jesus say: Now, I must go to Jerusalem and suffer, and I must be killed, and the third day be raised again? What would you have said? You would have said what Peter said, and so would I. I would have been wrong, I know. The Cross to Peter and to all of them meant defeat. How is He going to build His Church? How is He going to create an institution against which the gates of Hades cannot prevail? How is He going to commit to those who are within the Church the keys of moral interpretation to the world, if He is going to allow Himself to be done to death in Jerusalem?

The Cross terrified them, and I do not wonder at it. From that moment all the disciples were afraid. Follow at your leisure and watch them. From that moment at Caesarea Philippi these men were out of touch with Him. They still loved Him, they stood by Him "in all His temptations." What a wonderful thing it was He said, "Ye are they that have continued with Me in My temptations." [15] They had; but they could not understand Him. They were just frightened out of their wits at the Cross. The Cross was the end of everything. How can it be other than that, if He is going to put Himself into the hands of His enemies? (I am trying to think as they thought.) And when the Cross actually came, you have that tragic sentence, "They all left Him, and fled." [16] That is what the Cross did for Him and for the Christian movement. It scattered His followers as chaff is scattered before the sweeping of a simoom. All gone! The terror of it! I'm not surprised, are you?

It is very cheap for us to sit this side of Pentecost and criticize them. I do not know that the Church of God has even yet grasped the significance of the fact that her way of victory is through the Cross. All Peter saw in the Cross was a foul and brutal murder, and he was right in "minding the things of men" if that was *all* he saw. He was not minding the things of God. He had not seen the deeper meaning of it; and there he remained all the way for six months. Take the four Gospels and go over those six months. Again and again Our Lord took them aside and told them that He must go to Jerusalem to suffer and die. But He never once told them He was going to the Cross without at the same time telling them that He would rise again. There is not a single reference to the Cross that is not linked with the resurrection.

The marvel was that they did not seem to hear that. They were not impressed by the resurrection. Why not? Well, I think it was just a theological statement to them. The Pharisees believed in resurrection. When Jesus said to Martha, "Thy brother shall rise again" do you remember what she said? She said, "I know that he shall rise again in the resurrection at the last day." [17] By which she meant, That does not comfort me now. I want him now. She postponed, theologically, the resurrection. I think the disciples did that. I think that is why they did not seem to take much notice. It is so very significant that He never mentioned the Cross without linking it to the resurrection; yet they never seem to have heard.

So far, Peter was right. If there is nothing other than the Cross, if there is no resurrection, then the Cross makes me an infidel forever. If that life, so rare, so radiant, so beautiful, so pure, so true, is to be done to death, mauled by the hands of malice and hatred, and God does not interfere, then I have no belief in the goodness of God. Unless there is something other than that in the Cross, I am done with any faith in God. Perhaps that is what Peter felt.

Then came the resurrection, and that changed everything completely. Read the introduction to Peter's first letter, "Blessed be the God and Father of our Lord Jesus Christ, Who according to His great mercy begat us again unto a living hope by the resurrection." When they saw Him on the Cross, all hope perished. They were born again to hope when they found Him alive.

Now Peter, in his sermon, refers to the Cross and the resurrection. How does he do it? He does not begin with the human side of it, he begins with the mystery. "Him, being delivered up by the determinate counsel and foreknowledge of God" (but as far as you are concerned), "ye by the hand of lawless men" (that is, men without the law) "did crucify and slay." There are two sides, said Peter, to this Cross—the sin that murdered Him; and yet, enveloping that, is a mystery of divine determination and foreknowledge. *Now* Peter has seen "the things of God" as well as "the things of men." By the illumination of the Spirit he is no longer minding "the things of men"; he is minding "the things of God." There is a meeting in the Cross of the ultimate in human sin and divine grace. *I look at that Cross, and see sin doing its damnedest.* I look at the cross again, and I am in the presence of mystery.

> From the ground there blossoms red,
> Life that shall endless be.

In the mystery of the Cross I am finding the way into life.

And then we go on. "Whom [this same Person] God raised up, having loosed the pangs of death: because it was not possible that He should be holden of it." "The pangs of death." A great phrase, that! And then hear Peter's challenging cry, seeming to me to echo with victorious laughter that day, "because it was not possible that he should be holden of it." Resurrection!

In our next study we shall look at the parenthesis and see what that resurrection meant; *why* it was not possible that he should be holden of death; how death that day proceeded to resurrection, and how, through that resurrection He is exalted to be a Prince and a Saviour.

CHAPTER 7

ACTS 2:24-32

The whole of this paragraph to which we come in our consecutive series in this wonderful second chapter of the Acts, has to do with the central fact—the resurrection of Jesus. We have seen that there are three facts preceding the resurrection: the fact of His manhood, the perfection of His manhood, and His death; and three facts following the resurrection: His exaltation by the Father, His reception of the Spirit, and His bestowal of the Spirit. At the heart of it all is the resurrection.

Let us spend a moment examining the paragraph as to its structure. First of all a declaration is made: "Whom God raised up, having loosed the pangs of death." Then an affirmation. Notice the difference. Peter has made a declaration and follows it with a great affirmation of an exultant assurance of triumph. He says, "because it was not possible that He should be holden of it."

Then he turns aside in verses twenty-five to thirty-two, a parenthesis we called it, which is an explanation of his affirmation, or his defense of it, if you like. And he does it by quoting from one of the Psalms.

Notice how verse twenty-five begins: "For David saith concerning Him . . ." and he quotes from Psalm sixteen, verses eight to eleven, to prove the accuracy of his affirmation. Then, at verse twenty-nine he defends his use of the Psalm. Notice the logical sequence of all this. Why does he defend his use of the Pslam? Someone may have said, What right have you to take that Psalm and make it apply to Jesus of Nazareth? I say, someone may have said that. They are still saying it. Well, Peter tells why. He says, "Brethren, I may say unto you freely of the patriarch David, that he both died and was buried, and his tomb is with us unto this day." This Psalm, says Peter, celebrates Someone Who goes down into death, and emerges out of death. Therefore David could not have been talking about himself. He died and was buried, and we have his tomb still with us. Then of Whom was David speaking? Peter goes on to tell you:

"Being therefore a prophet,"—in this Psalm there is more than psalmody, there is prophecy—

Being therefore a prophet, and knowing that God had sworn with an oath to him, that of the fruit of his loins He would set One upon his throne; he foreseeing. . . .

Now comes the little word "this." It is not in the manuscripts at all, but the translators put it in, thinking something was needed there. Sometimes you have to put in an English word to fill up an idiom. But sometimes a hiatus is more powerful than the filling in of a gap:

He foreseeing, spake of the resurrection of the Messiah. . . .

(I use the word "Messiah" there purposely, because, as you know, "Christ" is merely the Greek form of "Messiah.")

He foreseeing, spake of the resurrection of the Messiah, that neither was He left unto Hades, nor did His flesh see corruption.

You see what Peter is doing. He is defending his use of the Psalm. He is saying that David could not have been referring to himself, because he died and was buried; but, he says, being a prophet, he knew something. What did he know? He knew that God had sworn with an oath unto him that of the fruit of his loins He would set One upon his throne; *knowing that,* he, foreseeing, spake of the resurrection of the Messiah, "that neither was He left unto Hades, nor did His flesh see corruption." Then Peter follows immediately by naming the Messiah: "This Jesus did God raise up, whereof we all are witnesses."

First, then, we have the declaration, "Whom God raised up." And because we are studying this very carefully we go back to what we know of the Person of whom he is speaking, "Jesus of Nazareth," the perfect One; His perfection demonstrated by the fact that God was able through Him to work the powers which were wonders and which were signs. "Him, being delivered up by the determinate counsel and foreknowledge of God"—that is the grace of the Cross; "ye by the hand of men without the law did crucify and slay"—the sin of the Cross.

"Whom God raised up, having loosed the pangs of death." I do not know any phrase more wonderful in its revelation or suggestiveness than that. Notice that in the Authorized Version, not inaccurately, but I think a little inadequately, it is rendered, "the pains of death." Let me state with all reverence and delicacy that the word means "birth pangs"; the birth pangs of death, and there you are in the mystery of the Cross. In His death there were birth pangs. New life was coming out of that death.

I do not think any interpretation is necessary there, nor would it be helpful. There are some things in your Bible that are really very, very wonderful; some phrases in both the Old and New Testament that today we hardly dare render literally.

I am going off on another excursus for a moment, as they say in academic halls. There are phrases which, if you translate literally, some people in this very respectable, refined and neurotic age, would not quite like. A minister told me not long ago that he never read from the pulpit the story of the Virgin Birth because it was not delicate. The man who objects to it on that ground must have a corrupt mind, and has no business in the ministry. There is in much of the language of Scripture a daring use of metaphors and figures that are startling, but if you just leave them as they are and let yourself think them through, you find yourself in the presence of something tremendous. Peter, speaking in the power of the Spirit on the day of Pentecost said, "Whom God raised up, having loosed the birth pangs of death," and I stand in the presence of a marvel and a mystery.

We pass on. "For," said he, "David saith concerning Him. . . ." Let us examine that quotation from Psalm sixteen. There are lots of things we might say about it. As I have already said, I am not preaching; we are just taking our way through the passage, working together as students. In reading this discourse have you ever turned back to that Psalm and looked at the part Peter was quoting? It is worth doing. One or two things you will discover. Let me name one, and do not be frightened by what I am going to say. Peter did not quote the exact words of the Psalm. But he did not alter the sense by a single touch. The sense is the same, but not the words. I wonder what you think of that—those of you who are so eager about verbal inspiration. You say to me, Don't you believe in verbal inspiration? It depends on what you mean by verbal inspiration. I say this to you, that no New Testament speaker, either Jesus Himself or others, quoted exactly from the Hebrew Scriptures. They changed the wording, but they never changed the sense. Peter here changed the wording slightly.

First notice in passing that this settles the authorship of Psalm sixteen. "David saith . . ."—so David certainly wrote this Psalm. I am quite certain he did not write all of them, but this one he *did* write. Whoever wants to take Psalm sixteen and put it at a much later date, is certainly out of court according to Peter's statement. Every argument breaks down here if David did not write the Psalm; because everything is based on the fact that he did so.

Notice that in the quotation, beginning at the eighth verse and running to the end of the Psalm, there are three descriptions. There is a description of life, a description of death, and a description of emergence out of death—of resurrection.

> I beheld the Lord always before My face;
> For He is at My right hand, that I should not be moved:
> Therefore My heart was glad, and My tongue rejoiced.

That is life.

> Moreover My flesh also shall tabernacle in hope:

"dwell in hope"—"tabernacle" is the marginal word. I am going to take another.

> Moreover My flesh also shall *encamp on* hope:
> Because Thou wilt not leave My soul unto Hades,
> Neither wilt Thou give Thy Holy One to see corruption.

That is death.

> Thou madest known unto Me the ways of life;
> Thou shalt make Me full of gladness with Thy (countenance).

That is resurrection. David there, in poetry, is describing Someone Who lives in a certain way; Someone Who dies; Someone Who rises; but he is describing the kind of life, the quality of death, and the necessary sequence of resurrection. The resurrection results from the quality of the death, and the nature of the death results from the character of the life. Peter says it is prophetic. He is describing a life, and he is putting into the lips of the Person referred to the words: "I beheld the Lord always before My face." That is life. But such a One is going into death, and of that experience He says, "Moreover My flesh also shall encamp on hope." When you have life of that quality, you experience death of that nature. What was the issue? The same Person is speaking, having been into death, "Thou madest known unto Me the ways of life." That is resurrection.

Peter says, "It was not possible that He should be holden of it." Why not? Well, says Peter, let me quote to you what David said. Now, David did not write that of himself. He died, and was buried, and we have his sepulchre. But he, being a prophet, foreseeing the One Who should sit on his throne, the One Who is to be Messiah, he "spake of the resurrection of the Messiah," that He should not be left to Hades, or see corruption. Why not? Because of the nature of His death, and *that* because of the nature of His life. Here cause and effect are seen in relation to each other in a marvelous sequence, the medium being a song of David, and the use made of it by Peter.

Now trace the effect to the cause. What is the ultimate issue? "Thou madest known unto Me the ways of life; Thou shalt make Me full of gladness with Thy countenance." But how is that so? That is resurrection. It is so because that resurrection resulted from the peculiar nature of the death. What was the peculiar nature of the death? "My flesh also shall encamp on hope: Because Thou wilt not leave My soul unto Hades, neither wilt Thou give Thy Holy One to see corruption." Here is the death which Someone undergoes knowing that death cannot hold Him, that God will not allow death to retain Him.

Well, what made Him so confident in going into that death? The kind of life He had lived. What kind of life was it? "I beheld the Lord always before My face; for He is on my right hand, that I should not be moved." When there was *that* life there was *that* dying, and where there was *that* dying there must be *that* resurrection. It was impossible that He Who had so lived and died should be holden of death.

Or put all I have said in another way: When you have a life of that nature, there is no place for death in it at all. But that Person *does* die; the fact of death is there. It follows that you must at once recognize that there is a difference in the death of that One from the death of any other. His death is different because His life is different. Where you have a life like that with a death like that, there is only one result possible. "It was not possible that He should be holden of it." There you have the text for Peter's sermon, and all the means to prove it.

The subject is resurrection, and Peter's argument and his use of this Psalm was in order to demonstrate its necessity. Let us confine ourselves entirely to the reasons for resurrection as set forth here. On this day of Pentecost, Peter did not attempt to prove the risen Lord by massing the evidence of those who saw Him afterwards. Paul did that in the fifteenth chapter of I Corinthians, where he cites the evidence of those who saw Him alive after He had risen from the dead. He names Peter, James, and the Twelve, then five hundred at once; and at last he says, "and . . . to me also." [1] Those were the historic proofs that Jesus is alive. In his conclusion Peter says, "This Jesus did God raise up, whereof we all are witnesses." So in this place Peter is proving the resurrection as an inherent necessity; it *had* to be.

Let us take our courage in both hands and state the thing clearly: If God did not raise Jesus, then He would be violating eternal principles. "It was not possible that He should be holden of it."

124

Peter is saying in effect, Jesus of Nazareth won a threefold victory over sin, and because of His threefold victory, death could not hold Him. What do we mean by a threefold victory?

First, He won a victory over the possibility of originating sin. That is not very clear, but we will come back to it. Secondly, He won a victory over sin as suggested to Him from without, as temptation. Finally, and because of these two victories, when He died He won a victory over sin as assumed responsibility. And when that threefold victory was won, death could not hold Him.

Take the first, victory over the possibility of originating evil. That is in the first line of the quotation, "I beheld the Lord always before My face." No other human being has ever been able to say that in the sense in which it is said here.

We must call to mind here the unique personality of Jesus. He was God's second Man; the Son of God Who, in the flesh, had assumed a new relationship to His Father. Now, put that fact in relationship to this. It is done for us finally and perfectly in the writings of Paul. In his letter to the Philippians he says, "Have this mind in you, which was also in Christ Jesus." [2] Then he goes aside to show us the mind of Christ: "Who, existing in the form of God," ("the form" meaning the method of manifestation) "counted not the being on an equality with God" a prize to be snatched and held for Himself, "but emptied Himself" (not, of course, of His Deity, but of that form of sovereignty), "taking the form of a servant, being made in the likeness of men." [3]

Keep those two thoughts together as you think of Jesus of Nazareth. A Man, Jesus, yes; but Who is He? He is the One Who had equality with God, Who has taken the place of the Servant of God, leaving the realm of sovereignty, and coming into the realm of submission. There is a depth of mystery here. For me at least, let me put it like this: I cannot talk about the death on the Cross, or the resurrection of Christ, or the atoning work of Christ, and think only of the Man, Jesus. That is impossible. I must always remember Who the Man is.

Look at the Man, Jesus, and remember what lies behind. The Son of God has taken the form of a servant. Am I not warranted in saying that there, in God's universe, is a new Being, on the angelic plane but not of angel nature? "He took not on Him the nature of angels;" [4] but took another plane of life, lower than the angels, and became a man, a servant. Here is a new Being. No angel is like Him. No man is like Him. He is sovereign.

What does this mean? Here is a Being, having taken the position of submission to God, and within that fact is the possibility of personal rebellion against God. Some of the angels did exactly that. I go for a moment to the epistle of Jude and to the sixth verse: "Angels that kept not their own principality, but left their proper habitation,"—that is not punishment, that is sin; the punishment follows—"He hath kept in everlasting bonds under darkness unto the judgment of the great day." I only want you to get that flash of light upon the sin of angels. What was that sin? They did not keep their principality; they left their proper habitation. Now we are in the realm of the mystery of evil; and insofar as your Bible reveals, the origin of evil is there.

Evil originated in the being or beings of angels. They were not tempted by other beings. They left their principality, their true habitation. In the fourteenth chapter of the prophecy of Isaiah, the prophet speaks of Satan. Notice what he says of him. "How art thou fallen from heaven, O daystar, son of the morning! how art thou cut down to the ground . . . ! And thou saidst in thy heart, I will ascend into heaven, I will exalt my throne above the stars of God; and I will sit upon the mount of congregation, in the uttermost parts of the north; I will ascend above the heights of the clouds; I will make myself like the Most High." [5] Evil originating in a personality which was not tempted from without.

I submit to you that the whole of that possibility is suggested in this, "I beheld the Lord always before My face." As though He said, I kept My habitation; I did not depart from the orbit of My self-chosen Servanthood to God. I did not revolt against the Divine government or seek to assume it. Keep these things in mind, and then at your leisure do what I can only hint at now. Listen to Jesus talking, " I spake not from Myself; but the Father that sent Me, He hath given Me a commandment, what I should say, and what I should speak." [6] "I do nothing of Myself, but as the Father taught Me, I speak these things. . . . I do always the things that are pleasing to Him." [7] "We must work the works of Him that sent Me." [8] "My meat is to do the will of Him that sent Me." [9]

Here is this Being, this Jesus, Who is God-Man, this One Who is of the eternal equality with the Father, having divested Himself of sovereignty and assumed the position of a servant; and in that very fact, is there not the possibility of the originality of evil within Himself? But—"I beheld the Lord always before My face." [10] Jesus never left His habitation. He kept His principality as it was appointed, the Servant of the Lord. No deflection there, no wish or will apart from the sovereignty of His God, sovereignty of which He had divested Himself. Angels were created, and some of them fell when in their hearts they said, We shall make ourselves "like the Most High." [11] Man was created, but that was a different creation. Man never stood where angels stood.

Now to the second victory. When you read the story of the fall of man, remember evil did not originate in the thinking of man. It came to him from *without*. He was tempted. There was no temptation of evil to Lucifer, son of the morning. It originated within himself. Man fell in response to temptation.

127

Now take the second phrase, "For He is on My right hand, that I should not be moved." [12] Not only was there no origination of evil within His Person, He kept His orbit, His habitation; yet He was tempted. He was tempted in all points like as we are; but, He said, The Lord at My right hand was the consciousness of My life, and I was not moved. I did not move of My own volition from My orbit. I did not move in answer to temptation from without. He never moved from loyalty by yielding to an attack, or failed to act in consonance with the One at His right hand.

I behold that Man, and go back to Peter's description, "approved of God by miracles and wonders and signs which God wrought through Him." Here is the perfect One, perfect in His lonely personality that put Him apart from angels, apart from men; the Son of God Who is the Servant of God; in His humanity never originating evil, never departing from His sphere, His orbit; He was tempted as man—for God was never tempted nor can be—without falling, when all the tides of evil swept upon Him." "The Lord is on My right hand, that I should not be moved," and He was not moved. There is the double victory.

Very well. Then what? "Moreover My flesh also shall encamp on hope . . ."—that is how He died. "Thou wilt not leave My soul unto Hades, neither wilt Thou give Thy Holy One to see corruption." Here is the mystery of death.

When I said that there was no place for death in His life, I meant that there was no need for such a One to die at all. What is death so far as man is concerned? Why do men die? You can make it a scientific inquiry if you like; I do not object at all. Get your scientific friend to tell you why men die, and do not be put off with a superficial answer. Get your theological professor to explain to you the reason why men die. Do not let them smile at you; press them until they tell you. Why do men die? Well, they will say, What do you mean by that? Of course men die. Why of course? Well, it is the natural order. Is it? Why is it the natural order? Well, in process of time the body deteriorates in the work of reconstruction. I was told when I was a boy that the body reconstructs itself every seven years. Today they are changing the length of that period a little. Do not misunderstand me. I speak with real respect for science. I was taught that if, for instance, you have a seven-year-old-boy in your home today, there is not a single particle of that little body that was there when the boy was born. The body rebuilds itself, takes in new material, casting off the old tissues. What I want to know is, why cannot that go on without ceasing? Well, says the scientist, as the years go by, in the reconstruction there is a little deterioration. The present reconstruction is not equal to the last. I do not need them to tell me that. I am in my ninth body, and I know this one is not as good as the last one, and the last one was not as good as the one before that. For years it rebuilt itself until one came to the center of virility, when it was almost impossible to get tired. Then it began to lessen. The old resilience and buoyancy were not there, and the next body will not be equal to this. Why? There is no apologist in the world who can answer that question. He can describe the process; he can tell you the vibrations are not what they were, and so on; he can analyze the blood ·and all sorts of things, but he can never tell you why men die. The Bible says it is because of sin, that the spiritual and moral have touched the physical at that point by a Divine fiat. "The soul that sinneth, it shall die." [13]

Well now, given a sinless One, along the realm of the natural, there is no place for death in Him. There was no need for Jesus to die. So far as He was concerned, His life came to its complete finality for this earth in the Mount of Transfiguration when He was metamorphosed. Not death but metamorphosis, for that is the Greek word behind transfiguration. He had neither in His own unique personality originated evil, nor had He yielded to the seduction of evil from without. His was a double victory over sin, and there was no place for death. But He died. And when He died, He died according to this word:

My flesh also shall encamp on hope.
For Thou wilt not suffer My soul to remain in Hades,
Nor allow Thy Holy One to see corruption.

Do you remember one of the most amazing things He said of Himself? "No man taketh My life from Me." [14] But it looks as though they did. Oh, no. "I lay it down of Myself." If I should say that, and were murdered tomorrow, you would have a right to laugh at me. But would you have a right to laugh at Jesus when He says that, unless—unless what? Listen, He has not finished: "I have *power* to lay it down, and I have *power* to take it again." And put over against it these words, "Thou wilt not leave My soul in Hades, neither wilt Thou give Thy Holy One to see corruption." In the death of such a nature, resurrection is inevitable. Then what is the meaning of this death? Why did He die? The answer is in the tenth chapter of John from which I have taken that quotation, "I lay down My life for the sheep. . . . the good Shepherd layeth down His life for the sheep." He took it again for His sheep. *Vicarious* dying—you cannot get rid of that word. The moment you deny that word in the presence of the death of Jesus Christ, then His death becomes for you only the death of an impostor, and for you He never rose. And, of course, if He never rose, you have no Cross. No man who denies the resurrection preaches the Cross of Christ. He cannot do it. He must get rid of the Cross, except as the martyrdom of a man, unless he acknowledges the resurrection.

And so you now have a threefold victory; the last being His victory over death as responsibility *assumed*. He "bare our sins in His body on the tree." [15] He assumed responsibility for sin He had not committed. That death created a moral value in the universe that was valuable to other people. By His very dying, Who need not die, there is a value created in the economy of God which is valuable to me. Death is the issue of my sin. Death is the dissolution between my body and my spirit. Death is separation from God. His death is for me; if He never rose, then my preaching is vain, and your faith is vain, and we are left in our sins. He rose because of that threefold victory: victory over the possibility of originating evil within His own personality, victory over evil as it assaulted Him in temptation from without; victory over evil as He assumed the responsibility for it in His dying. "Whom God raised up," said Peter with magnificent defiance, "having loosed the pangs of death: because it was not possible that He should be holden of it."

That resurrection is the keynote of the Christian Gospel. If Christ won that threefold victory, then death could not retain Him. He felt its pangs, but they were birth pangs. If Christ rose He did so because He had won that victory.

Did He rise? The answer is in your soul and mine. Documentary evidence? Yes, any amount of it. There is no event in history more clearly proven on historic grounds than the fact of the resurrection of Jesus. And yet, as to its application, that is not enough. That He rose is proved in the fact that in your soul and in mine He is winning His victory over sin, breaking its power, cleansing us from its pollution—not only in the eyes of men, but in our own inner heart and conscience. The victory of our Lord in death was the reason for His resurrection, and His resurrection is the demonstration of that mighty final victory wherein He, assuming responsibility for sin, put sin away by the sacrifice of Himself.

131

CHAPTER · **8**

ACTS 2: 33-36

Being therefore by the right hand of God exalted, and having received of the Father the promise of the Holy Spirit, He hath poured forth this, which ye see and hear. For David ascended not into the heavens: but he saith himself,

The Lord said unto my Lord,
Sit Thou on My right hand,
Till I make Thine enemies the
footstool of Thy feet.

Let all the house of Israel therefore know assuredly, that God hath made Him both Lord and Christ, this Jesus Whom ye crucified.

Those are the last sentences in this wonderful address, the first delivered in the power and light of the outpoured Holy Spirit.

In a certain way it may be said that all revelation is focused in this chapter. When John added the postscript to his Gospel that we call Chapter twenty-one, he said, "There are also many other things which Jesus did, the which if they should be written every one, I suppose that even the world itself would not contain the books that should be written." [1] Some people smile when they read that, and think that John had become a little excited, and they say it is hyperbole. Oh, no, it is not. That is cold scientific fact. Because if you were to record all that Jesus did and said, with its ultimate meaning, you would have to write a book on every blade of grass that is found on the hillside.

We are following this description of a process: Jesus, a Man, Jesus, the perfect One; Jesus in His death; Jesus raised by God out of death, because it was not possible that He should be holden of it. Now we take it up right there.

"Being therefore by the right hand of God exalted. . . ." In that phrase we have the next stage, the risen Jesus, ascended to the right hand of God. The meaning is not that it was an act of God, although it was that, but that Christ is at the right hand of, or by the side of God. Peter does not name the ascension; now he assumes it. He has named the resurrection, the risen One is ascended, and he now sees Him at the right hand of God exalted.

"And having received of the Father the promise of the Holy Spirit. . . ." That in a phrase is the next stage in the movement. And then the final one, the great, the climacteric to which everything has been moving to interpret the day of Pentecost, "He hath poured forth this, which ye see and hear."

Then Peter turns aside again to quote a Psalm in preparation for the final thing. All that has gone before is explanation. The last movement in the address is proclamation. To introduce that proclamation he turns to a Psalm:

For David ascended not into the heavens: but he saith himself,
    The Lord said unto my Lord,
    Sit Thou on My right hand,
    Till I make Thine enemies the
    footstool of Thy feet.[2]

Let all the house of Israel therefore know assuredly, that God hath made Him both Lord and Christ. . . .

Mark the "therefore" linking the proclamation with that word of David to which we are coming in a moment. "Let all the house of Israel *therefore* know assuredly. . . ." That is the proclamation; that is the way the sermon ends. And then, in order that there be no mistake, in order that no one listening may ever forget, Peter swings back and says, ". . . this Jesus whom ye crucified." It is the same Person, Jesus, all the way through.

Now, in that wonderful little phrase, "Being therefore by the right hand of God exalted," we are called to think again of the ascension. It would be a good thing if we could, just now, take a few moments and try to visualize the ascension of our Lord, not from the earthly side merely, but from the heavenly side, to see the ascension, not as they saw it who lost Him to sense and sight, but as they saw it who saw Him arrive in Heaven.

In the first chapter of this book of Acts is the account of the Ascension as it concerned that little band of disciples. He led them out of the city, and when He had uttered those words, "Ye shall be My witnesses," Luke says, ". . . as they were looking, He was taken up; and a cloud received Him out of their sight." That is all. Now, quietly, for a moment or two, follow Him. Remember, He did not cease to be Jesus then— He was still Jesus of Nazareth. He was not, to use a phrase I have used before, dissipated into thin air. Jesus of Nazareth was lost to sight to those watchers on the hillside, as they saw Him moving away from the earth in bodily form, and the cloud receiving Him. Can we follow Him?

Of course there is a sense in which language must break down or perhaps become inaccurate. We know so very little, necessarily, of the conditions that lie beyond this present life.

All we know, we know by revelation and by faith, and faith can travel a long way, though it goes haltingly, for we do not know. There are dimensions you and I know nothing about yet. There must be. Einstein has told the world that, scientifically, there is another dimension—a sixth. He says himself that there are not six men in the world who can understand it, and I am not one of the six! But we realize that there must be other dimensions and laws. We talk of locality, and of course there is locality, there is place. To what place Jesus ascended, and how He moved to it—all these things are entirely beyond us. For instance, space and time have a relativity that we do not always recognize. The light that you see from the sun today—how long ago was it starting from the sun before you saw it? You are seeing things now that according to our timing, happened long ago. Do you see? The light that you see now left the sun a long time ago.

The Hebrew people thought and spoke of three heavens, and you find references to them in your Bible. Paul says he was caught up into the third heaven. That is no figure of speech. Young people become poetical and talk about the seventh heaven. I have been in it, too! But the Hebrew never talked about the seventh heaven, and quite intelligently. To him the first heaven was the atmosphere surrounding the earth; the second heaven was the whole area of space, the stellar spaces, immeasurable of course, the spaces in which suns and stars and planets swing in rhythmic, eternal order. And the third heaven was the place where is the supreme and central manifestation of the glory of God. Three heavens. That is what Paul meant when he said he was caught up to the third heaven, beyond the heaven of the atmosphere, beyond the heaven of the stellar spaces. Whether that word "beyond" is right, I do not know. Paul did not use it. I am using it because I do not know the laws which govern these dimensions, so I am happily agnostic in these matters. But that is the idea. When Jesus said, "Behold the birds of the heaven," [3] that is the first heaven. When you read in your Bible about the stars in heaven, that is the second. When you read about the place of Divine manifestation where the angels are, and the spirits of the just, that is the third. As to whether you have to pass in ways that you and I talk of when we speak of crossing continents and oceans, as to whether we pass through the heaven of the atmosphere and the stellar spaces to find the third heaven, I do not know. I am not anxious about it. I shall get there when He takes me. That is all that I'm concerned with. But it *is* a place, and to that place Jesus of Nazareth ascended. He is there now. He has not lost His human form and never will, for God has taken humanity in Jesus into eternal being and relationship with Himself.

Very well, then. With all these hinted or expressed limitations of thought, "being at the right hand of God exalted" means that the risen Man of Nazareth has ascended to that central place of Divine manifestation at the right hand of God. Now that is where I would like to pause. I like to imagine that I am there when He arrived. There were spirits of men there. Moses was there, and Elijah was there, and Abel was there, and Abraham was there; and a great host of others. But when He arrived, a Being arrived in heaven such as had never been there before. Not one. All of humanity that had arrived before He came, were there by the mercy of God. He did not come by the mercy of God. He came in the inherent right of His own sinlessness. If there had not been other high work on hand for Him to do, He might have gone there from the Mount of Transfiguration. If it had been merely a case of His own sinless humanity, as we said before, in that metamorphosis He was prepared to pass right out into that heaven then and there. But now there came to Heaven a Man, God's exalted Man. This was God's thought when He said, "Let us make man." [4] I believe that the watching angels were filled with rapture when He came. Angels had watched Him all His earthly life, and under Divine command had ministered to Him. They came to the wilderness when He was tempted. One of them came to Gethsemane; they were always ready to serve in the Divine will, but were withheld in His self-abnegation. They had watched the first man, Adam, and some had guarded the way to the tree of life with the flaming sword. Now they see this Man come, and all the hosts of those who were there by the mercy of God see Him come. And in my thoughts I am in that company. I look at Him and say, This is the Man, the exalted Man.

But why are there wound-prints visible in the hands and feet of this Man? You and I know the answer. He comes not merely in the perfection of His manhood, but having accomplished on His Cross an exodus. I am not imagining this. On the holy mount He talked with Moses and Elijah about the exodus He should accomplish. He has beaten down the gates of brass, and cut the bars of iron asunder. He has left a highway along which men and women, in spite of sin and failure, may pass and come where He has gone. He has done more. He has historically—if I may use the word in such a realm as this—created a right on which, and on which alone, Abel and Enoch and Noah and Abraham and Moses and the others could remain in heaven. It is a daring thing to say, but sometimes we have to run these risks in order to express ideas on the human level; but *if He had failed,* these must have left the heavenly places. For the Lamb was slain from the foundation of the world in a Divine purpose. Now the thing is done. On Golgotha's rough and rugged cross one great shout came from His lips. In a loud voice—mark that well—came one word. We need three to translate it. "It is finished!" [5] Now He has ascended, God's Man, yet in His wounds representing all who had failed according to the Divine purpose and intention. At the right hand of God exalted. The Man of Nazareth.

Now Peter, in a participial phrase, describes the great enactment: "Having received of the Father the promise of the Holy Spirit." What can that mean? That Man of Nazareth was a Man of the Spirit. Follow through the life story of Jesus and you behold a human life entirely dependent upon the Spirit of God. Conceived of the Spirit in a unique and wonderful way. Facing His public ministry, we are told that He was full of the Spirit. When He was about to be tempted, we are told that He was led of the Spirit, or driven by the Spirit—I am using phrases from the different evangelists. He executed His ministry in the power of the Spirit; and we learn that it was "through the eternal Spirit He offered Himself to God." [6]

Then what does this mean that He "received . . . the promise of the Holy Spirit"? In that phrase we must go back to the time when, as Luke records in his Gospel, he said to these men, "I send forth the promise of My Father upon you." [7] In the first chapter of Acts it is recorded that He told them to "wait for the promise of the Father," [8] the coming of the Spirit —the Spirit promised by the Father.

Someone may say, Where was that promise made? Go back to the Old Testament. Isaiah has it in his forty-fourth chapter: "I will pour My Spirit upon thy seed." Joel, the prophet already quoted, has it: "I will pour out My Spirit upon all flesh." You cannot read Ezekiel without discovering it there in the figurative language he uses to describe the river, the foretelling of a day when the Spirit should come. Jesus at the feast of tabernacles said, "If any man thirst, let him come unto Me and drink. He that believeth on Me . . . from within him shall flow rivers of living water." There is the link with Ezekiel; and John adds, "This spake He of the Spirit, which they that believed on Him were to receive; for the Spirit was not yet given, because Jesus was not yet glorified." [9]

With reverence and a great consciousness of the limitation of language, I affirm that it was an official act of God when

He, the Man of Nazareth, passed into the heaven of heavens in the perfection of His humanity; Who nevertheless was wounded because of His having borne away the sin of the world. He received the Spirit from the Father in all fulness, not for Himself but for all whom He represented.

I know that in the presence of this great act of God we are trying to see heavenly happenings by our consciousness of earthly procedure. We have no other way. But it does remain a fact that it is a Man of our humanity, Jesus of Nazareth, Who passed into the heavens and received the gift. "In the beginning was the Word, and the Word was with God, and the Word was God . . . and the Word became flesh." [10] There in humanity is incarnate Godhead, representing us.

Do not forget our consideration of Joel. When, through the Man of Nazareth the Spirit was poured forth upon those waiting disciples, and made them one life with the risen Lord, He was also poured forth upon all flesh to convict of sin, of righteousness and of judgment. It is a great thing for us who are believers to go over that passage often, and just watch the great Divine program working itself out, and see what the coming of the Spirit really meant. He had come many times in the Old Testament days, but always as a visitor. There was no abiding in human souls, no resting on humanity. But on the day of Pentecost, because of that Presence in the glory of the Man at God's right hand, He received the Spirit, and He received the Spirit representatively. He was representing me. That sounds selfish, I know, but put yourself in there. There are some things you have to put in the first person singular. He loved *me*, He gave Himself up for *me;* for *me* He rose, for *me* He ascended, for *me* He received the Spirit, for *me* He poured that Spirit forth. There is the great and wonderful procession.

The great argument of this declaration concerning Jesus is that everything was of God. God demonstrated His perfection through His works. God delivered Him to death. God raised Him from the dead. God exalted Him to the throne. God gave Him the Spirit for those He represented and for all humanity. The whole redeeming movement is here—the revelation of the victory of grace. Sin put Him on the Cross, and there is no activity of man after that. Did you notice it? Man drops out. But God's Man proceeds, and as the result of His reception of the Spirit He creates a new race, a new human race. How does He do it? By taking hold of the members of the fallen race and giving them new birth, new life, making them members of Himself. That is the meaning of Pentecost. Sin refused His manifested perfections, trampled under foot His teaching. Cities refused to repent. A feverish, restless and silly childish age (I am using the words because Jesus said, "They are like unto children . . . in the market place,") [11] refused His message, and sin put Him on the Cross. Grace gave Him to the world. Grace demonstrated His perfection. Grace delivered Him to the Cross. Grace raised Him from the dead. Grace exalted Him. Grace gives Him the Spirit for the very people who had rejected Him, and He, in grace, "shed forth this." That is Peter's last word in answer to the inquiry of a city, "What meaneth this?" That is the answer we have to give to men when they ask us the real meaning of our Christianity.

Peter then quotes from Psalm one-hundred and ten, and makes his proclamation.

> For David ascended not into the heavens: but
> he saith himself,
>> The Lord said unto my Lord,
>> Sit thou on My right hand,
>> Till I make Thine enemies the
>> footstool of Thy feet.
> Let all the house of Israel therefore know assuredly. . . .

Then the proclamation: "That God hath made Him both Lord and Christ, this Jesus Whom ye crucified." Let us take the declaration itself, and the Psalm quotation in a moment.

May I draw your attention—for we are doing close work here—"God hath made"? I want you to notice that actual word. "Let all the house of Israel therefore know assuredly, that God *hath made* Him both Lord and Christ." That is a simple verb, the verb "to make," but here it indicates a single act, a crisis. Once again you have to visualize in your earthly and human thinking, a procedure of heaven. There is a historic value here that harmonizes exactly with that passage in Philippians to which I have referred, that tells of the self-emptying of Christ: "Who, existing in the form of God, counted not the being on an equality with God a thing to be snatched and held, but *emptied Himself,* taking the form of a Servant, being made in the likeness of men; and being found in fashion as a man, He humbled Himself, becoming obedient unto death, yea, the death of the Cross. Wherefore also God highly exalted Him, and gave unto Him the Name which is above every name; that in the Name of Jesus every knee should bow, of things in heaven and things on earth and things under the earth, and that every tongue should confess that Jesus Christ is Lord, to the glory of God the Father." [12]

Do you not see the relationship between that great word of Paul and this word of Peter? "Being by the right hand of God exalted . . . He hath poured forth this. . . . God hath made Him both Lord and Christ, this Jesus." There is the act, the great act of God in its place in history.

Of course, God has always been acting in history. When He called Abram it was an act in history. When Jesus was born it was an act of God in history. Now in that sequence of history, a Man is made Lord and Christ.

"Made Lord." That does not mean that He had not been

Lord; but that at last the hour had come in which the inherent superiority of this Man is to be placed central to the whole universe by God on behalf of humanity. Thus the inherent Lordship of Jesus is ratified.

Not only Lord but "Christ." You and I are so familiar with these titles that we read them with their spiritual value in mind, yet sometimes without intellectual apprehension. May I turn aside here and say especially to my young friends: It would be a big task and demand a great deal of watching, but go through your New Testament and mark the naming of Jesus. He is called Jesus, He is called Christ, He is called Jesus Christ, He is called Christ Jesus, He is called the Lord Jesus Christ, He is called Christ Jesus the Lord—all sorts of groupings. I submit this to you; there is always a reason for the grouping, and in the context you find the reason. There is only one name—Jesus. Christ is not a name; it is a title. Lord is not a name; it is a title. And the grouping of these names is full of suggestiveness.

(In the same way the names of God in the Old Testament are suggestive. That is one reason why you will be helped in reading the American Standard Version, where the word Jehovah is used for the tetragrammaton instead of Lord. We will use this word again when we come to an instance of it in a moment in Psalm one hundred and ten.)

So, whenever you are reading, watch whether your Master is called Jesus or Lord; there is always a reason for it. That is not merely a guess on my part. It is the result of many years of study. "He hath made Him Lord"—personal supremacy, "and Christ"—official supremacy. And to know what "Christ" means, you are bound to go back to the Old Testament. Do you know where that title first appears in the Old Testament? I love to discover these first occurrences. In the first book of Samuel, and in the second chapter, you find the prayer-song of Hannah:

My heart exulteth in Jehovah;
My horn is exalted in Jehovah.

That is how it begins. How does it end?

Jehovah will judge the ends of the earth;
And He will give strength unto His King,
And exalt the horn of His Anointed.

"His Anointed"—His Messiah. In the Septuagint Version it reads, "His Christ," which means His Anointed. That is the first idea of the Messiah that obtains in the historical books. It is in the song of a woman—which opens up another little side exercise for the Bible student. Someday read Hannah's song and Mary's magnificat. Put them side by side and compare them. This woman, Hannah, way back there in the twilight, is singing a song about her baby to come, and as she sings her soul is climbing up on that little baby-life and seeing great things. She sees the Christ. Now whether she quite understood what she sang I am not sure; whether she was merely thinking of her Samuel I cannot tell; but she spoke the name, the Anointed, the Christ. I go on through this Old Testament and I find the Christ idea repeated—the hope, the aspiration, the prophecy, the sob, the sigh, the song about the Christ. It always has in it two ideas: one, king; the other, priest; and those two ideas merge. The Hebrew conception of Messiah, not always emphasized on both sides, even by prophets and singers, was of One in Whom two offices are merging, the kingly and the priestly. Messiah wears a crown, but His crown is the mitre of the priest. He wears the ephod of priesthood, but with the purple of royalty. And the great hope of Messiah-Christ in the Old Testament is the coming of One Who shall redeem and reign as Priest and King. Peter says here that God has made Him Lord and Christ. But, you say, He was Christ before.

143

He surely was. But now the victory is won and everything is completed. When He was born on earth, God sent an angel to tell them to call His name Jesus; when He was exalted Paul says that God placed that name above every other name—that in the name of Jesus every knee should bow. The great procession and the great sequence.

Now here is Peter, declaring in Jerusalem for the first time that God hath made Him Lord and Christ. He is Lord, the sovereign One; He is supreme. Beyond His dictate there is no appeal. God's eternal sovereignty is vested in the Man at His right hand. He has also made Him Christ, and I am constrained long enough to say, Hallelujah! The One Who is vested in eternal sovereignty is the "Lamb as it had been slain." [13]

What is this that God has done? He has crowned humanity at the center of the universe. This is Jesus of Nazareth, Lord and Christ. Holiness is crowned, for He was the sinless One. There is no lowering of a standard. Sacrifice is crowned. Victory is crowned, for the resurrection is the demonstration of victory won. Authority is there, invested in that Man. Fellowship with God, for He received of the Father the Spirit—"the Spirit of truth, which proceedeth from the Father." [14] The eternal procession of the Spirit from the Father to the Son, and through the Son poured out upon that company. And the result was power. Let us leave that word without any qualifying adjective, because there are some things that, when you qualify, you minimize. Power as well as authority is vested in the Man at God's right hand. He hath made Him Lord and Christ.

Now to go back to the Psalm from which Peter introduced that great declaration. He says, "For David ascended not into the heavens." You see, he is picking up where he left off. In quoting from Psalm sixteen he had reminded them that David died and was buried, and they had his tomb; therefore he could not have been speaking of himself there. Now he goes to another Psalm, Psalm one-hundred and ten, and quotes the phrase, "David ascended not into the heavens." Do you see the significance of that? It does *not* mean that David, in his spiritual personality, had not gone to heaven. It means that his body had not. David died. He passed on with Abraham and Isaac and Jacob and the others. You remember when the Sadducees came asking Jesus a question, He said, "God is not the God of the dead, but of the living," [15] and He was talking about Abraham, Isaac, and Jacob. They are neither dead nor asleep; they are alive. That is what Jesus meant.

If David died, then, he could not have said about himself:

> The Lord said unto my Lord,
> Sit Thou on My right hand,
> Till I make Thine enemies the
> footstool of Thy feet.

Why did Peter quote that Psalm? Do you not think it was because he had heard Jesus quote it? How long before? Oh, perhaps seven or eight weeks before. The story is in the twenty-second chapter of Matthew. Just before His Cross, Jesus was talking to the rulers in the Temple. He entered the Temple on three consecutive days, and on the last day the rulers came and asked Him, "By what authority doest Thou these things?" [16]

They came with other questions on another occasion. The Pharisees came with the Herodians and asked a question. That is significant. They represented two opposing political parties. The Herodians believed that the yoke of Rome was good, and that you should obey the emperor and pay your taxes. The Pharisees paid the taxes under protest. They did not believe it was right to pay taxes to Rome. Now they made a coalition, and I am always more or less suspicious of political coalitions. They came together to Jesus and said, "Is it lawful to give tribute unto Caesar, or not?" [17] You remember the marvel of our Lord's answer: "Render therefore unto Caesar the things that are Caesar's, and unto God the things that are God's." That is the perfect philosophy of a man who believes in God in relation to his state, country, or government.

Immediately afterwards the Sadducees, the rationalists in religion, came with their question about a man and his wife: "In the resurrection therefore whose wife shall she be?" [18] A theological question, and the Lord went behind their stupid illustration to the bedrock of their rationalistic outlook, and said, "God is not the God of the dead, but of the living." He told them that in heaven they neither marry nor are given in marriage, and gave them that fundamental, theological answer.

Then there came a lawyer with an ethical question. He saw that Jesus had put the Sadducees to silence, and on behalf of the Pharisees he said, "Which is the great commandment in the law?" [19] Jesus answered, not by quoting from the decalogue, but by the use of one commandment which included all the rest: "Thou shalt love the Lord Thy God. . . ." Three questions—political, theological, and ethical.

Then He asked them a question, "What think ye of the Christ?" [20] And mark this. *"The Christ"* there was used officially—What is your opinion of Messiah? "Whose Son is He?" He asked it of these men who knew it all, who were supposed to know everything about that sort of thing. Why, they said, the Son of David, and they were quite right. Now, He said, I ask you, If He is David's Son, how is it that David calls Him Lord? And He quoted the very words that Peter uses right here:

> The Lord said unto my Lord,
> Sit Thou on My right hand,
> Till I put Thine enemies underneath Thy feet. [21]

He says, How is it that David calls the Messiah his Lord, if Messiah is his Son? They could not answer Him—or they would not. To answer would have been to admit that He, Messiah, was more than the Son of David. Our Lord was not playing tricks with them; He never did that. He was giving them another opportunity to reconsider the truth about Himself.

Peter, quoting the same Psalm, says, "David . . . saith himself, The Lord said unto my Lord. . . ." Now here is a case where the translation leaves us a little befogged. I turn back to Psalm one-hundred and ten and read it from the American Standard Version, "Jehovah saith unto my Lord. . . ."

We have two different titles there: "Jehovah . . . my Lord"; the latter being "Adonai," which means "the sovereign Lord."

There are three supreme names for God in the Old Testament; they are Elohim, Adonai, and Jehovah. In the English Bible, Elohim is rendered "God"; Adonai is translated "Lord"; Jehovah is usually rendered "Lord," but the American Standard Version of 1901 helpfully transliterates the name as "Jehovah."

May I remind you of what I said about this previously? The Hebrews expressed that name "Jehovah" in manuscripts by four letters, YHVH, the tetragrammaton. If a rabbi were reading, he substituted another name out of reverence. It was a mistaken and wrong reverence, but in the use of the King James Version we are suffering from the same mistake. We do not know or see the difference, except in typeface: "Jehovah" is Lord; "Adonai" is Lord.

"Jehovah saith unto my Lord"—Adonai, sovereign Lord. All Jewish interpreters have made this Psalm Messianic. Now, said Jesus, how is it that David's Son was called Lord by him? How can David call Him Lord? It needs the eastern mind to understand that. *Your* son may rise high, and you may call him Lord, but no eastern father would. The father there is never inferior to the son. Never. Well then, how is it? There is only one answer—because this "Son" was the Lord of David in the inherent fact of His Personality. That is what Jesus was driving these men to discover: that according to their own Scriptures their Messiah would be more than the son of David; He would be the Lord of David; Lord of David in the deepest fact of His nature and being—the very Son of God as well as Son of man.

"Therefore know assuredly, that God hath made Him both Lord and Christ." Not merely by the inherent superiority of His human life, but by the eternal sovereignty of His Person: He is the Lord and He is the Christ.

That is the proclamation that Peter made on the day of Pentecost. The crowd had said, What does this mean? He had interpreted it to them—that they had seen the thing fulfilled which their prophet foretold. He had described the great and wondrous procession of events, all massed within one high period of time, when Jesus came—perfect, dying, risen, ascending, receiving, pouring out.

This is the thing I have to say to you, says Peter, that God hath made Him, this Jesus, both Lord and Christ. That is the Christian message to the world at all times. That is our message to the world today. That is the all-inclusive witness of the Spirit. That is the real Pentecostal proclamation. That is the inclusive witness of the church to the world; that for which, and for which alone, the church can claim Pentecostal anointing and Pentecostal power; it is to proclaim Him Lord and Christ.

I sometimes feel that the great lack today, even in evangelistic work, is that we have not a sufficient sense of sin. One of the last things that William Ewart Gladstone, that great British statesman of the late Victorian era, said in public utterance was this, "The malady from which England is suffering today is a lost sense of sin." That was a great word from a statesman. Do you say, You are getting old and out of date? Well, my memory of evangelistic work in bygone days is that men and women were brought under conviction of sin, and it meant real business. You say, Why does that not happen now? May I say this without being misunderstood? One reason is that we are a little too eager to preach Jesus as Saviour. What! you say, too eager to preach Him as Saviour? Yes, I think so. I think our first business is to present Him as Lord; and when men and women are brought into the presence of the Lordship of Christ, then they will know their need of a Saviour. Thank God, He *is* Christ also. We can preach Him as Saviour, but we need to get back to a presentation of the Lordship of this Christ. That was the Pentecostal declaration.

CHAPTER • 9

ACTS 2:37-47

In this paragraph we have the results, immediate and continuous, of the things we have been considering as revealed to us in this wonderful second chapter of the Acts.

First, the immediate results of the coming of the Spirit, the creation of the Church, and the testimony of one witness standing in that new life, and speaking for the whole Church. The Spirit, the Church, and the preacher—that is the great relationship; we miss everything if we miss that. The preacher in the midst of the Church; the Church and preacher filled with the Spirit.

Well now, what was the result? Here we are back, as I said at the very beginning of our studies, at the springs in the hills whence the rivers have proceeded. In this passage we have the account of the *immediate* result, contained in verses 37 to 41. In verses 42 and 43, we find the *continuing* result: "And they continued stedfastly in the apostles' teaching and fellowship, in the breaking of bread and the prayers. And fear came upon every soul: and many wonders and signs were done through the apostles." From verses 44 to 47 Luke describes the outward movement, the *enlarging* result of the thing that happened that day.

If we could have a week of studies in this paragraph alone,

we could only touch the suggestiveness of it. Here are the lines, here are the standards, here are the measurements, here are the weights, the acid tests of the Church of God, all about her work and the conditions of membership both for entry and for all continuing conditions. Everything is here; if only we could bring our church life back to this test, what a great thing it would be for God and the world! "Judgment must begin at the house of God," [1] beloved. Before we see any great movement in the outside world, there will have to be a great movement inside the church, a return to the laws and principles and power of the Holy Spirit. So as we study together technicalities of the text, I pray that the very breath of that selfsame Spirit may move over the page, and that we may see and understand these things, and be led to conform ourselves to them.

Let us, then, enumerate and summarize the immediate results of Peter's preaching. First, conviction and inquiry produced in the hearers. "They were pricked in their heart"—conviction; and they said, "What shall we do?"—inquiry. You notice that the question of the crowd has changed. When first they were arrested and amazed they said, "What meaneth this?" Now they say, "What shall we do?" That is conviction and inquiry. The next thing is instruction and exhortaton. To use a more modern term, the aftermeeting began now. When the preaching was ended, and the people said, "What shall we do?" Peter went on to give instruction and exhortation.

His instruction: "Repent ye, and be baptized every one of you *upon* the name of Jesus Christ unto the remission of your sins; and ye shall receive the gift of the Holy Spirit." Then exhortation: "For to you is the promise, and to your children, and to all that are afar off, even as many as the Lord our God shall call unto Him. And with many other words he testified, and exhorted them, saying, Save yourselves from this crooked generation." So you see that this went on for some

151

little time. Peter is giving clear and definite and explicit instruction. I do not think three thousand people came all in a rush. I think there was a period to give opportunity to the halting and hesitating ones. In that period of instruction and exhortation more and more came, and the crowd grew.

The third immediate result was the obedience of these who received the instruction and exhortation, and their addition. "There were added in that day about three thousand souls."

To go back. First, "They were pricked in their heart." What was that pricking of the heart? What was the conviction that came to them in that moment that made them ask the question, "What shall we do?" What had Peter declared? What was the great climacteric in his discourse? He had traced the prophecy of Joel to the present happening; he had traced the cause in the life of Jesus of Nazareth; and he had proclaimed that, "God hath made him both Lord and Christ, this Jesus Whom ye crucified." Observe two notes in the proclamation: the Lordship of Jesus, and the sin of those who crucified Him. They were convinced of two things, the Lordship of Jesus and of their own sinfulness. How was this conviction produced? By a double witness—the witness of the Holy Spirit and the witness of a man. We are trying to see principles while we are looking at technicalities. The Spirit and a man have borne witness to convince a crowd. A little later Peter said as much: "We are witnesses of these things; and so is the Holy Spirit, Whom God hath given to them that obey Him." [2] Peter preached, the crowd heard, and while they were listening, perhaps quite unconsciously to themselves, Another was taking the truth and bearing it in on their hearts, and that Other was the Holy Spirit. How does that affect you, those of you that preach, whether as regular preachers or lay preachers? To me that is one of the great secrets of rest and comfort in preaching, that whereas I have to think and prepare and speak as though everything depended on me to make the thing plain to those that listen—for that is my responsibility—yet while I preach, if I am in right relationship with my Lord, the Holy Spirit is making it plain to people, apart from and beyond my preaching. Yet He needs the human voice and the man in order to do his work. What a wonderful union! What a wonderful thing it is for the preacher to realize this holy co-operation, the man and the Spirit witnessing together! These people were convinced first of the Lordship of Jesus, and therefore of their own sin. "What shall we do?" How shall we relate ourselves to Him as Lord? How shall we deal with the sin of which we are conscious? That is the great cry of convicted souls.

Now I ask you to look very simply, as Bible students, at Peter's answer. What did Peter say? It is not only interesting, it is very valuable; because, if we are going to do evangelistic work, whether specialized or in the regular work of the Church, inevitably men and women will say to us, "What shall we do?" We have heard your testimony; what shall we do to get right with God? What about our sins? What must we do to enter into this life of the Church?

How are you going to answer that question? When someone comes to ask you what he or she is to do in order to enter into that holy fellowship, and into that joy, and into that relationship with that Lord in spite of sin, what are you going to say?

I must tell you that one of the things that fills me with alarm in these days is the loose and easy way in which evangelism is sometimes carried on in regard to its aftermeeting and decision work. I tread with very great care here, because God does fulfill Himself in many ways. I am not saying that this kind of approach to people is not accomplishing results, but I think it might do greater and mightier things if it got back to some very old-fashioned methods—I mean the methods of the Bible. Sometimes people are told, Oh, all you have to do is just to shake hands with the evangelist and everything will be all right. That is the thing that is ruining evangelistic work! Just come and shake hands, and if you would like to join the church we will put your name down on the roll! The Church of God needs safeguarding from that kind of thing. We have let down the bars. We have made the thing too cheap. In an unholy passion for statistics we are weakening the spiritual power of the Church in the world. I pick up a religious paper, and I read that some man is spoken of as having the biggest church, the largest membership, or the largest Sunday school in a certain area. God bless you, but don't advertise that. That does not mean that your church is spiritually powerful. It may be, but it may not be. I have known some little churches in great cities, down in a difficult quarter, which are the real centers of spiritual power in the neighborhood and district.

Let us get back to what Peter said. He said, "Repent." Do you say that? If you do not, you are not delivering the Christian message. If you say, Only believe, you are not delivering all of the truth. You can say that to a man only when you see that he is repenting. When the Philippian jailer, scared out of his wits, and feeling after spiritual things, came crying to Paul and Silas and said, "Sirs, what must I do to be saved?" [3]—that man was repenting already. Paul said, "Believe on the Lord Jesus Christ, and thou shalt be saved." [4] But the first word is "Repent."

What is it to repent? Change your mind, that is what the word means. You say, I thought it meant change your conduct. You will never do that until you have changed your mind. "As a man thinketh in his heart, so is he." [5] Repentance goes down to the root of motive, to the inspirational center of life and thought. "Let the wicked forsake his way, and the unrighteous man his thoughts." [6]

I will not stay to discuss here the long continued controversy between the Roman and Protestant theologians. It all clusters around two words for repentance found in the New Testament, "repoenitere" and "poenitentiam agite." One word means sorrow, pain and penitence; and the Roman theologians say that is the real meaning. The other word means to change the thinking, the mind; and the Protestant theologians say that is the real meaning. And they are right. In every instance where repentance is given as a condition for entering into the experience of salvation, the word means a change of mind, a change of front. I once heard D. L. Moody say, "I will tell you what repentance is. A man is going that way, and a voice behind him says, Halt! Right about face! Quick march! That is repentance." But he does not even halt until he makes up his mind to change his direction. Change your mind, then everything follows—conception, conduct, character.

What next? "Be baptized,"—I am reading now from the King James Version—"be baptized every one of you in the name of Jesus Christ." Both the King James and the American Standard Versions give it that way up to this point. "for the remission of sins," says the King James; "unto the remission of your sins," says the American Standard. Now listen carefully as I word it another way, "Be baptized every one of you *upon* the name of Jesus Christ." Someone says, Why do you do that?

Now for a little technical classroom work. The difference is simply the difference between two Greek prepositions. One is the word *en,* as we would spell it. That means *in.* The other is the word *epi,* which means *upon.* Now which preposition is used here? Of course you know that there is not in existence an original document of a single book in the Bible. But there are manuscripts and translations, and we have many more manuscripts available today than when the King James translators did their work. Many manuscripts use the word *en* here, but some of the oldest use the preposition *epi,* upon. Now which is right? Nobody can be dogmatic as to which is the word Peter used, because both words are used in different manuscripts. In such a case as this we must decide by getting the sense of the whole passage. If the preposition there is *en*, what does this mean? "Repent and be baptized every one of you *in* the name of Jesus Christ." If that is so, this is the only place where baptism is referred to as being *in* the name of Jesus Christ. Christian baptism is never *in* the name of Jesus Christ. The formula of Christian baptism is found in the words of our Lord, "Baptizing them *into* the name" [7]—and the word is *eis*, another preposition. If this word is *en,* it contradicts that.

Do you say, That does not matter much? I beg your pardon, everything matters much. If *en* is correct it means that there is baptism in the Name for remission of sins. Now, there are those who hold that view; but it contradicts all the rest of the New Testament. I will not stay giving manuscript quotations or reasons. However, I believe I have enough evidence to bring me to the decision that the text is *epi* there. "Be baptized every one of you *upon* the name of Jesus." Now, that Greek preposition that I have translated "upon" means more than something resting on; it means *"depending on."* That is the force of the word. We have incorporated the word "epi" into the English language in such words as epidermis, epiglottis.

I was once dealing with this word, and later had a letter from one of the most eminent surgeons in Chicago, in which he said, "I was intensely interested in your definition of that passage, and I am convinced from my standpoint it is inevitable." He went on to tell what "epi" meant in the medical use of it—not lying upon, but *identified with* by lying upon. That is the meaning here, without a doubt to my mind. "Repent and be baptized every one of you *depending upon* Jesus Christ unto the remission of your sins." If you say, *"in* the name," faith is not chronicled there at all. All you have left is repentance and baptism, and that contradicts the whole teaching of the New Testament. Here is the formula: The order of experience is that first you depend on the name of Jesus Christ, and then you are baptized. With what result? First, the remission of your sins. Secondly, you shall receive the Holy Spirit.

Here is the answer to people today who say, "What shall we do?" Change your mind; depend upon Jesus Christ, upon His name; confess Him, breaking with the world by open and definite confession and by baptism.

We are simply examining a Biblical passage. I have no axes to grind—I flung them away years ago. I represent no ecclesiastical polity or theology. I never signed a creed in my life and I never will, not even the Westminster confession or the new Fundamentalist confession. But I will sign the Bible every morning, noon and night. I do not want any Baptist or non-Baptist to get anxious about me. So far as I am concerned, I believe in immersion as a baptismal confession of faith and practice. As a Congregational minister I had a baptistry at my church at Westminster, London, and a font by the side of it. If people wanted their children baptized by sprinkling, I did it. None of my children was ever sprinkled, but I have used this mode for other children at the desire of their parents. I am not going to be forced into a quarrel with people on secondary matters, nor on post- and premillennialism. Real fundamentalism, if you want to know what it is, is a belief in the Deity of Jesus, and the Cross of Jesus as man's only hope. There are many other things that we can talk about, agree or differ about, and then shake hands and sing, "Blest be the tie that binds." That is my attitude, and I want that to be understood.

If in the process of time we have amended, or if we have any right to amend, any form of that process—repentance, belief, confession, and baptism, the open and public confession of a break with the past—it must not be the repentance and it must not be the faith. Whether it is baptism, I leave you to decide. I do not think it is necessary to salvation, but repentance is, and faith is.

Repent, believe, confess. That is all you can do. Well, but what about my sins? You have remission of sins; that is God's act. What about my new life? You have the Spirit—the entrance to the holy fellowship from the beginning.

Peter went on to exhort and testify. What happened then? "They then that received his word." Notice that it *is* his word, what he had said, and what they believed and obeyed—they "were baptized"; baptism being the outward confession of their belief and obedience. What then? "And there were added unto them. . . ." In the American Standard and King James Versions the words "unto them" are printed in italics, which means that they are not in the Greek text, but supplied by translators to give help. You say, But it means "unto them." Yes, secondarily it does, but not in the first place. Let your eye run on down to the forty-seventh verse and you find the expression again, "And the Lord added to them. . . ." Well, you say, it does mean that they were added to them. Yes, and in the King James Version it says that they were added to the Church. But the first thing is that they were added *to the Lord,* and because they were added to the Lord they were added to "them" and to the Church. I do not want to appear hypercritical, but I do love accuracy, because I think it helps us to understand. Our business is not to get men and women added to our membership roll. That is a secondary thing. Our business is to get men and women added to the Lord; then it will follow that they will be added to the Church and to our statistics. When were they added? When they received the word and publicly confessed; when they were obedient. Here are the first results: They obeyed, they received, they were baptized, they were added. It was a growing movement, primarily united to the Lord and therefore to the membership.

Now we come to a little verse, a wonderful verse, so characteristic of Luke. Luke knew how to put a great deal into a verse. He put twelve years in the life of Jesus into a verse:

And the child grew, and waxed strong, becoming full of wisdom; and the grace of God was upon Him.[8]

Then he put the next eighteen years into a verse:

And Jesus advanced in wisdom and stature, and in favor with God and men.[9]

Here he gives us another verse:

And they continued stedfastly in the apostles' teaching and fellowship, in the breaking of bread and the prayers.[10]

There is the new Church order. When people joined that Church then, it meant business. The conditions of entry were radical and revolutionary—repent, believe, confess. Their whole life was changed.

"They continued stedfastly." That is a tremendous word. It denotes a new attitude of life. Life is gathered up, life is intensified, life is devoted, life will now be lived with passion and power. "They continued stedfastly." They did not treat the thing cavalierly. They did not join the Church as a man joins a club, just to drop in when he feels inclined. That is what many are doing today, all over the country—joining the Church as though it were some sort of religious club, and sometimes it is not the "religious" that attracts them. Just join the Church and drop in when you like. Come down to the oyster supper! No. I am serious about this. I think that is one place where our weakness lies. When those people in Jerusalem were added by the Holy Spirit to that holy communion it meant something.

"They continued stedfastly in the apostles' teaching and fellowship, in the breaking of bread and the prayers." I would like four studies with those four things. "They continued stedfastly in the apostles' teaching." What does that mean? It means that they put themselves under instruction, and held themselves together. They did not imagine they were able to take strong meat and do a man's work all at once.

How I would like to have been in that early company! Yet I need not feel that, because I have all the apostolic teaching in the epistles—twenty-one letters in the New Testament. Go through the letters and you will find two elements in apostolic teaching—doctrine and duty. They are never separated; truth and triumph, creed and conduct, they are always together. Apostolic teaching always kept them together, showed their interrelationship.

Take Paul's letters. Notice that in every one of his letters there is one great central "therefore." You will find the word "therefore" scattered all through, for his was a logical mind. He was always showing cause and effect. But in every letter there is one great "THEREFORE." He lays out the scheme, and shows the application of doctrine to duty. Take Ephesians, the great doctrine of the Church—her predestination, her edification, her vocation. Then in chapter four: "I *therefore*, the prisoner in the Lord, beseech you to walk worthily of the calling wherewith ye were called." Then he gets down to the business of application; the Church must walk worthily as husbands and wives, parents and children, masters and servants; it is doctrine and duty all the way through. Take his great Roman letter with all the spacious arguments of Salvation. Then in chapter twelve: "I beseech you *therefore*, brethren, by the compassions of God, to present your bodies a living sacrifice, holy, acceptable to God, which is your spiritual worship." Doctrine and duty. "They continued stedfastly in the apostles' teaching." They put themselves under instruction. How many church members are doing that with the men who are placed in oversight in spiritual things?

What next? "Fellowship." Now do not put that word "fellowship" in the same category as teaching. In fellowship as well as in teaching is the practice of communion. The Communion Service, you say? No, that is coming presently. That word "fellowship" is one of the greatest and richest words in the New Testament. The Greek word is "koinōnia," so rich in its suggestiveness that you will find it translated in many ways: fellowship, communion, distribution, contribution, partnership, partakership—all translations of the one word. What does it mean? What is its root? Further on, in this very paragraph, is the root from which it comes. It says in verse forty-four that they "had all things common,"—"koinos." Do not associate that always with the material. It was expressed in that way; but it is the having of *all* things in common. What happened to these people? What happened to you and to me when we were joined to the Lord? We had all things in common with God; all God's resources placed at our disposal; all our resources placed at His disposal. What about tithing? Tithe if you like. It is a sacramental symbol, but it is a poor business. *All* is at the disposal of God!

These people continued stedfastly in fellowship. The material expression is named later, but I am more anxious to stress the spiritual. It means that they talked together of the things of the Spirit; they compared with each other their experiences; they had fellowship in conversation, in communication, in spiritual things. Now that, beloved, is almost a lost art in the Church today. Fellowship. And here I am going to utter an ecclesiastical heresy, not a doctrinal one. I believe that no church ought to be so large in its membership that all the members cannot know each other. A fellow-minister tells me that he has a membership of 1800. Altogether too many! They cannot possibly all know each other. If you have a membership as large as that, break it up into groups. Let me address my Methodist friends. John Wesley, that great seraphic statesman-saint, who was so much ahead of his age that every modern spiritual and forward movement in Methodism that is worthwhile is a return to the spirit and genius of John Wesley. What did he do? He gathered his people together in Society Classes. There was the secret of the strength of Methodism. If you are not following this program today you are losing the great genius that made the Methodist Church a mighty thing.

Many years ago, in Birmingham, England, I sat in the study of a man I have always held to be the greatest in the Congregational order. (Remember, Congregationalism is an ecclesiastical position, not a doctrinal one; that is always so.) He was Robert William Dale who wrote that monumental work on the Atonement. He said to me, "You know, Morgan, if I could do it, I would graft the Methodist Class Meeting onto the Congregational system, and I would make attendance at it obligatory to membership." It was a tremendous thing to say. But why? I am not talking about a certain form of Class Meeting. I know that everything can degenerate. The Lord's Supper can degenerate until there is nothing spiritual in it. Certain people go to Class Meeting and say exactly the same thing every week: "I thank God I am where and what I am; and when I started out on this good way I determined to see it through to the end. I have had many ups and downs, principally ups." That is not what John Wesley meant by a class meeting. In his class meetings they gathered together and talked of the things of their inner life, of their failures and their victories, and of their Lord; there is so much in that. Fellowship. What do we know about the life of fellowship in spiritual things today? Is it not an amazing thing that some real Christian people—and I am not questioning their Christianity—when they get together, talk about anything except their Lord. They talk about the weather, they talk about politics, but they cannot talk about the Lord. What a great thing it would be if we had gatherings in which we met not to pray. That is what I said, *not* to pray. Not to study the Bible—and you know I am not undervaluing that—but just to look into each other's eyes and talk about the inner life.

There was a day, even before Jesus came, when some men and women had found out the value of it. In the last of the prophetic books you read, "Then they that feared Jehovah spake one with another; and Jehovah hearkened, and heard." [11] To what? To their praying? No, they were talking to each other. What were they talking about? They were talking about the Name. They "that feared Jehovah, and that thought upon His name." The Hebrew language is very pictorial. Our language is poorer in this respect. "The Lord hearkened and heard." That sounds like a repetition of the same thing. The word "hearken" literally means "to prick the ears" as a horse does. Now I know it sounds a little strange, but I am going to say it. The Lord pricked His ears. There is a certain beauty in that idea. And it goes on to say that the Lord "heard." Now that is not to prick the ears; that is to bend down so as not to miss a word. The great Hebrew prophet is attempting pictorially to show God's sensitiveness when some of His people get together and talk about Him. The Lord pricked His ears, and bent down so as to miss never a word. Reading on in that third chapter of Malachi, at verse seventeen, "They shall be Mine, saith Jehovah of hosts, Mine own possession in the day when I act." [12] In the day when I act; not in the day when I make up my jewels, my possessions, but My jewels in the day when I act—they shall be Mine. Who? People who have been in fellowship together about My name. I would like a whole hour's study on this one subject.

What next? "The breaking of bread." That was the supreme priestly act of the Christian church from the beginning. Priestly? Yes, if you will remember that the first function of the Christian priesthood is not intercessory. I am resolutely going to use an unusual word. It is "eucharistic." It is an English word borrowed from the Greek and means "thanksgiving"—giving thanks and worship and praise. I would always call the Communion Service the Eucharist. You say, That is High Church. Then I am the highest High Churchman in the world. I believe in the real Presence, not in the bread and wine, but in His people. The Communion Service, the breaking of bread, is strictly an act of worship. It is the supreme act, the act in which we remember Him and show forth His death until He come. Thus the Advents are united by the ceremony.

> Thus that dark betrayal night
> With the last Advent we unite
> By one long chain of living rite,
> Until He come.[13]

My dear friend, you do not come to the Table of the Lord to confess sin. Your business is to do that before you come, or else stay away. You do not come to the Table of the Lord to pray for anything. You can do that elsewhere. You come to give God what He is waiting for, pure adoration. The first function of the Christian priesthood is eucharistic. It is praise and adoration. All these principles are in the Old Testament as well. "Whoso offereth the sacrifice of thanksgiving glorifieth Me." [14] The trouble is that we have almost lost the art of pure praise.

One other thing—"prayers." Now there I must pause. The word covers the whole realm of prayer; and again one could wish for a whole study period. In the New Testament there are ten different words for prayer, indicating the different methods in prayer and the different values of prayer. There is one word that means asking as a pauper asks, with empty hands, on the basis of grace alone. There is another word that means demanding as due in fulfilling certain conditions. There are words that mean talking familiarly together, waiting until God talks to you. But, someone says, God does not talk to men as He did to Abraham. Is there not another way of putting that? Is it not more true to say that men are not listening for God as Abraham did?

"They continued stedfastly in . . . the prayers." The whole company maintained, in all its activities, relationship to God. Apostolic teaching—they put themselves under instruction; fellowship—they cultivated their new life, exchanging their thoughts; the breaking of bread—the high eucharistic act of worship; prayers—all the exercises that held the soul in right relationship with God. That was the early Church.

Then the continuing results. We are told of these in the next paragraph. Those early Christians felt the compulsion of the spiritual to be so great that they said none of the things they possessed were their own. "They sold their possessions and goods." The exact meaning of the Greek here means their moveable property and real estate—and they divided it all up? No, they did not; do not misinterpret that. They simply put the whole thing into one resource, and as a man needed, so he received. There are those who say that that was where the Church made its first mistake. I say the Church made its mistake when it departed from it. At least we can appropriate the spirit of it. What is that? That inside the unity of the Church there should be no man or woman or child in need. No member suffering alone or rejoicing alone. "They had all things common."

What else? Fear. "Fear came upon every soul." The outside world said in effect: Here is a society and a condition that we must touch cautiously. If we ask these people what to do, they are going to tell us to repent and believe and be baptized and come under discipline. A holy fear fell upon all.

"And many wonders and signs were done through the apostles." Power, that is, force. Fear and force. So it began.

This is still the day of the Spirit. The Spirit has not changed. The Christ has not changed. The laws are not changed. If anything is changed, where lies the change?

CHAPTER · 10

ACTS 2

As we come to the last of these studies, my purpose is to attempt to summarize, for our profit, their spiritual values. We have worked our way through this chapter stage by stage, with something of attention to detail, yet it has only been in outline. The chapter is by no means exhausted. Some of my listeners may be exhausted, but the chapter is not. It is still waiting for us to go back to it, and I would like to feel that this page of the Divine oracles remains with you always; that there may be some who will take weeks and months to work through it again, word by word, breathing its spirit.

We chose the chapter because it gives the first account of the history of the Christian Church, the birth of the Church, and the first things that took place on that first day. It runs a little over that, because in the final paragraph a summary covers the days and weeks and months following, indicating the lines of the movement. Referring to my illustration from George Borrow at the beginning, we are like those who have climbed the mountain heights to the places where the springs are bubbling up, and in course of time become rivers. I never come back to this second chapter of Acts without thinking of that illustration. I pray therefore that we may not only have examined the origins of the great tide and stream of church movement and responsibility of which we form a part, but also that the result of our studying together may be that we shall have drunk more deeply of that life-giving stream itself. Such is my desire.

The chapter lies open before us. I want now to consider it in two ways. I want first to speak of the new facts following Pentecost, and of the difference that Pentecost made, the changes that were wrought—to gather it up and state it in a new way. Then, in the light of this chapter and our consideration of it, I want us to consider the limitations of the Pentecostal age, the age that dawned that day; for let it be recognized that on that day a new era *did* dawn in the history of the world.

I love to follow the Divine outlines of history as the Bible reveals them. I like that phrase—outlines of history. The amazing thing to me is the widespread popularity, even among supposedly Christian people, of such books as H. G. Wells' *Outline of History*. I cannot understand how any intelligent person with the Bible in his hand, and a knowledge of it in his mind, could have patience to do more than glance over the beginnings of that monstrosity.

In the Bible we have God's Outline of History. There is much the Bible does not tell. It begins with a cosmic sentence; it admits a catastrophic upheaval; then it tells you that God created man. From that moment all it has to do with is man, from the moment of his creation. Here in Acts 2 we have a piece of that history. The historic sequence of the Bible runs in this way: Genesis, Exodus, Numbers, Joshua, Judges, the Samuels, the Kings, Ezra, Nehemiah—there is the historic sequence, the outlines of history in the Old Testament. All the books I have left out are collateral writings, throwing light on this period. Then follows the Biblical silence of four hundred years between Nehemiah and Jesus. Then another sequence begins lasting about sixty-six years; the first thirty-three years or thereabouts, the life of Jesus, Matthew, Mark, Luke, and

John, running parallel, reveal that period. Just a generation as we measure generations in the history of the world, but that *central generation* in God's history of humanity. Then, in this book of the Acts a second period of just about the same length in time, approximately thirty-three years, between the crucifixion, resurrection and ascension of our Lord, and Paul in prison. It is not a full history. It is an account which illustrates that period. The writer is not telling you *all* that happened anywhere, but he has outlined the whole movement, and the historic fact is recorded. It is the beginning of that fact that we have been considering. We have been studying a new departure of God in human history.

Looking back over the past, these departures are all clearly marked, the points at which God came anew into fresh activity in human affairs. He has been doing it again and again. I do not mean by that that any method failed, but that one method always prepared the way for the next, and when the fulness of time emerged, the next came. Watch these Divine methods.

Here, in this second chapter of Acts a new day dawned in human history. Something took place in that little strip of country whose shores are washed by the great sea, that little country upon which all intelligent people are keeping their eyes today. There is no spot in the world that is so full of interest at this very moment as the land we call Palestine, the Holy Land. Take a map of the world, and consider the centrality, geographically, of that one small strip of land to the whole world. It is at the very center, and I say to you all, keep your eye on Palestine; keep your eye on Jerusalem. God has not done with Palestine; God has not done with Jerusalem. We have been looking at something that took place at that geographical center. We have been observing that remarkable event in Jerusalem, its effect upon the city, the preaching that followed and the results following that preaching.

What are the facts in world history that began there that

168

day? The answer is along three lines: the new facts as to Christ Himself, the new facts as to the Church, the new facts as to the world. What difference did Pentecost make as to the Christ Himself, as to that company of people who became His Church, and as to the world at large?

Then I want to speak of the limitations of the Pentecostal age, the age that dawned then and has continued for more than nineteen hundred years. That seems a long time to us, does it not? Do not talk about long times and short times when you are thinking about God's plans and methods. Modern punctuation measures that Pentecostal age by a comma. Go back to Nazareth when Jesus in the synagogue quoted from the prophet Isaiah [1]: "He hath anointed Me . . . to preach the acceptable year of the Lord." [2] [Jesus suspended the reading of this passage . . . at the comma in the middle of Isaiah 61-2.] He did not continue with the next phrase, "and the day of vengeance of our God." He gave the scroll back to the attendant. That "day of vengeance" has not come yet. It is coming. "The acceptable year of the Lord" is now. It dawned when He came. That was the first flush of the morning. He came out of the night to the accompaniment of angels' songs and the investigation of shepherds. And in the course of a brief thirty-three years the day of Pentecost came.

First, then, what difference did Pentecost make to the Christ Himself? Let us remind ourselves of the things in this great action of God in Christ which had been consummated *before* Pentecost. We have looked at them in detail as Peter, in his wonderful sermon, portrayed them in a sevenfold movement. In His last discourses to His disciples, Jesus said, "I came out from the Father, and am come into the world: again, I leave the world, and go unto the Father." [3] I think that no sentences that ever fell from His lips are more inclusive than those regarding His own mission. Two things had been accomplished before Pentecost. The incarnation was now an accomplished fact in history. Now—and I am going to use a word that I have used before—the "exodus" is accomplished.

Now, we say that before Pentecost two things were accomplished: the incarnation and the decessus, or decease—the exodus. That leads us to see the meaning of Pentecost and the real value of it. Two things were completed—the incarnation and the exodus. Let me put that in another way: two things were completed—the revelation and the redemption. In His incarnation He was the Revealer; in His exodus He was the Redeemer. The revelation was completed in those years of His earthly life. Seen by so few people at the time, there came into the world the complete revelation of God and of man—now, do not be startled at the completion of my sentence—and of the devil. In the lifetime of Jesus, taking it in its entirety, so little but quite enough, you have all you need to know about God and man and the devil. Satan was dragged out of his hiding place and we know him because we see him up against that Person. Paul once said, "We are not ignorant of his devices." [5] Sometimes I am inclined to think that I *am* still ignorant of his devices, and yet I know I am not if I have seen Jesus; for the devil has no avenue of approach to "Man-soul" that was not laid bare in the wilderness. Evil was compelled to express itself, flung up against the background of that Personality. John, in the prologue of his Gospel says that there was always light, and that the darkness has not apprehended it. "Apprehended" [6] there means "extinguished." The darkness had never been able to put the light out. John says, "There was the true light, even the light which lighteth every man, coming into the world." [7] Jesus, the light that lighteth every man, coming into visibility as the revelation of God, of man, and necessarily of all the dark underworld of evil, opposed to God and opposed to man. Light came when He came. Certainly the rulers did not understand it. Certainly His disciples did not. They did not know all the meaning of the light in which they were living and walking in those three and a half years. Certainly His own mother and His brethren did not know, there in Nazareth, all of its meaning. But it was there; it was focused; it was Divine revelation.

I go again to John's prologue and he says this, "No man hath seen God at any time; the only begotten Son, Who is in the bosom of the Father, He hath declared Him." [8] It is a great word, "declared," but it falls a little short of the tremendous significance of the thing that John wrote there. Once more I am going to take the Greek word that John used and not translate it but transliterate it into English form. "No man hath seen God at any time; the only begotten Son, Who is in the bosom of the Father, He hath exegeted Him." [9] Now, to many of you I can understand that that does not mean very much; but there is not a preacher who has not grasped it immediately, if he knows his business. What is exegesis? It is the bedrock of all preaching, leading to exposition. The Christian preacher is not a debater of doubts in public; he is not a speculator within the realm of his own rationality or mentality; he is a preacher of the Word of God. If he is doing his work properly he is an exegete, bringing out the thing that is there, that it may be seen and understood. Not reading into the word something you and I think it ought to mean, but bringing out what is in it.

John says that Jesus is the Exegesis of God, the Interpretation of God. The revelation was final; nothing has since been added to it. Nothing else has been said about God except the things He said, and by what He was. Incarnation brought revelation: the Cross, the Resurrection, and the Ascension—the whole way of redemption. In the mystery of the Cross He bore the sin of the world; in the might of resurrection He came from underneath the intolerable and incalculable mystery and burden of that Passion, victorious over the sin He bore. When He ascended, He passed into heaven as the Man

171

of Nazareth, in the right of His Manhood and in the right of His atoning work. Now I ask, What then did Christ gain when he poured out the Spirit? What place does the Spirit take in His work?

I answer by saying that by the outpouring of that Spirit, His redemption was administered in the experience of those to whom the Spirit came. By that outpouring the revelation that had been localized and focused right there in that little country was multiplied through that company of disciples and throughout that growing group which became the Church. This is the Divine purpose, the Divine intention, the Divine ideal, and the Divine meaning; the Divine power, in the coming of the Holy Spirit.

So far as Christ was concerned, the pouring out of the Spirit meant the administration of His redemption. By the coming of the Spirit, the value of His Cross, the victory of His resurrection, and the virtue of His ascension were beginning to operate in the lives of these people as they had never done, nor could, while He was with them in bodily presence. From the standpoint of our Lord, it is the great administrative beginning.

Bear in mind again the great cry that came out of the heart of Jesus upon one occasion: "I came to cast fire upon the earth; and what do I desire? Would that it were already kindled! But I have a baptism to be baptized with; and how am I straitened till it be accomplished!" [10] That was before the Cross, before the exodus. He was the Revealer, but He could not cast the fire until He had passed through His passion baptism. Now the exodus is over. He has passed through that passion baptism and the ascended Lord is no longer straitened, because now, on the basis of what He has wrought in the will of God, He has poured forth the Spirit, He has scattered the fire. The hour has come when the administration of His redeeming work is possible in the souls of men. The revelation that He had given to the world was multiplied in all the men and women who from that moment were to live one life with Him, and consequently were to go out into the world to reveal God to men. That is the meaning of the Christian Church.

Peter, writing about the Church said, "Ye are an elect race, a royal priesthood, a holy nation, a people for God's own possession. . . ." (Now, there is your purpose. Whatever you are, says Peter, you are those four things. For what reason?) ". . . that ye may show forth the excellencies of Him Who called you out of darkness into His marvellous light." [11]

The Church is the abode of Christ; and immediately after Pentecost, away they went. Go over the list of places named in this second chapter of Acts. It would be an interesting study to see where this crowd of people came from. Parthians and Medes and Elamites, and the dwellers in Mesopotamia, in Judaea and Cappadocia, in Pontus and Asia, in Phrygia and Pamphylia, in Egypt and the parts of Libya about Cyrene, and sojourners from Rome. Get your map and see from whence they came and to what country they returned. Has it ever occurred to you that one result of the day of Pentecost was that Saul of Tarsus went to Damascus? What made him go to Damascus? Quite evidently the work of Jesus Christ was growing there. He would not have left Jerusalem if there had not been a very remarkable manifestation of the Christian movement in Damascus. How was it started? You have no account of an apostolic visit. Much later Paul the apostle was extremely anxious to reach Rome. What did he want to go to Rome for? To plant a church there? Oh, no. The Church was there before he went, and he could not get there for a long time. Those Christians were so important to him that he wrote a letter to them, the letter to the Romans. How did that church get there? On the day of Pentecost there were "sojourners from Rome." The revelation that was local in Palestine, was focused in a Person, and by the administration of the Spirit was multiplied in the company who went out.

That is a very solemn consideration. That is the meaning of the Christian Church. That is what Christ gained. His mystic Body was born; the Body of Christ is the multiplication of His individuality by all believing persons—men and women, youths and maidens, bond and free. He gained the enlargement in spiritual power of His own realm of operation in revelation, and in such fellowship with Himself as brings His redeeming power to touch humanity everywhere. He had completed the revelation that no one at first had understood. He had completed the redemption that no one up to that point had entered into and shared. But when He received the gift of the Spirit from His Father, and poured it forth, then that redemption was administered in the souls of those receiving it, and that revelation was enlarged in the sphere and possibility of its operation in the world.

Closely allied is our second line of consideration. What happened that day as to that company of people? Let us glance back for a moment to Luke's previous treatise; that is, to his Gospel, at the twenty-second chapter. The time was Passover. Passover and Pentecost are separated by fifty days. Jesus is talking to His disciples. "You shall say unto the master of the house, The Teacher saith unto thee, Where is the guest-chamber, where I shall eat the Passover with My disciples?" [12] "The Teacher" . . . "My disciples." There they are at Passover, before the Cross. Do you see them? He is the Teacher. They are disciples. I run my eye down that chapter, and come to verse twenty-seven. He is still talking to them. "For which is greater, he that sitteth at meat, or he that serveth? Is not he that sitteth at meat? But I am in the midst of you as He that serveth. But ye are they that have continued with Me in My temptations." [13] I will come back to that. Further on, at verse thirty-five He says, "When I sent you forth without purse, and wallet, and shoes, lacked ye anything? And they said, Nothing." [14] And so on. Do you see the threefold relationship referred to which existed between Jesus and His disciples before the Cross? They were His disciples, they were His comrades, they were His servants. And for all that ministry of our Lord for three and a half years, those words applied. They were His disciples, He was the Teacher. They were His comrades who stood by Him in all His temptations. (I am bound to go aside here and say that I never read that, beloved, without feeling the wonderful grace of our Lord's heart; because it does seem to me that they were not particularly loyal to Him at times—*but He knew their hearts.* You and I judge them by little deflections and breakdowns and proofs that they were not as close to Him as they might have been. Yet He said, "You have stood by Me in all My temptations.") They were His comrades. And then He says, "Did I not send you?" They were His servants. Their relationship of three and a half years is illustrated in that final reference at the Passover feast. Peter, James, John, and the rest, they had stood with Him, they had worked with Him, they were His servants. Some of them He called "apostles." And the word, "apostle" means not only or primarily "one sent," but "one separated and then sent."

What difference did Pentecost make? Did they cease to be disciples? No. Did they cease to be comrades? No. Did they cease to be servants? No. He *did* say to them before He went, "Henceforth I call you not servants . . . but . . . friends" [15]; but they did not cease to be servants. Then, what change did take place for them? At Pentecost they became, as they had never been before, actual sharers of His very life. They were made one with Him.

Now, beloved, here is a great theme for Christian people. We are told that, at this point, we are in the realm of mysticism. What do you mean by mysticism? If you mean "mirage," no. But we are in the realm of mystery; of something in Christian life and experience that had never been in the world before. That group of men and women began to live one actual life with the Son of God. There was communicated to them a new life that they had never had before.

Some people have difficulty with this. They say, What do you mean? Do you mean to say that Abraham was not born again? Abraham never was, and never will be a member of the Church of God. But Abraham received Divine life, and with all those sons of God in the past, was brought to God by the activity of God. They had a new life, but not the Christ life. What those people on the day of Pentecost received was the Christ life, and that life is the Divine and human merged in one.

You cannot study your Bible without seeing that the Church is a Divine entity in itself, and does not cover the whole ground of divine operation. There were the saints of old. There will be others who are brought into the place of eternal relationship with God—all of them through the Cross. But it was the Church that was born that day, the very mystical Body of Christ whose final function will not be in this world at all. She *has* a function here, but her final function is in the ages to come, and in the heavenly places. You have never read the last teaching about the Church until you have followed Paul all the way from the fundamental letter to the Romans, to the last—Ephesians and Colossians: the Function of the Church and the Glory of Christ. What is to be the function of the Church? She is to be an instrument, in her union with Christ, through which angels are to be taught the wisdom of God, and the ages to come are to learn His exceeding grace and love and tenderness. Touching upon these things is not enough. I would like to stay much longer here. But you have your New Testament and can do so for yourselves.

Those men that day became more than disciples, but nonetheless disciples; more than comrades, but nonetheless comrades; more than servants, but nonetheless servants. They became members of Christ Himself. That is the most wonderful fact in all human history. Through the atoning work of the Son of God, the coming of the Spirit on that day of Pentecost made those human lives one life with the Son of God. They became members of Christ. They were added to the Lord.

I want this fact to be left indelibly on your mind. They continued to be disciples, but with a new capacity and a new vision. Until now they had stood outside Him and listened to His teaching, but they had never fully understood it. They tell you that after His resurrection they found out what He meant. Within half an hour of Pentecost, Peter learned more about Jesus than in all the three and a half years before. He was no longer outside. He had a new vision; the gift of the Spirit meant, and still means, a new capacity for discipleship.

Let me tell you a story. There was a good woman in England some time ago who suddenly became very wealthy. She had a daughter, and put this girl under the instruction of one of the great music masters, telling him, "Now, I want her to learn to play the piano." After about two months the master sent for the woman and said, "Madam, I cannot teach your daughter any more." "Why not?" she asked. "She cannot be taught to play," he answered, "because she has no capacity for music." "Then," said the woman, "buy her one. I have plenty of money." What is the philosophy of that story? If the child has not the capacity, you cannot buy it. But the Holy Spirit will *give* you the capacity for knowing the deep things of God. In that moment at Pentecost they received this capacity, because Christ was there by His Spirit within them.

"We have the mind of Christ," [16] said Paul. What a daring and magnificent thing! The "nous," the mind, the consciousness of Christ; that is what came to those men that day. Disciples, yes, but with a new capacity, a new vision, Christ within by the Holy Spirit, interpreting Himself to them. That is the final Christian evidence.

177

You cannot prove to anyone that Christ is Messiah by all your dialectics. You cannot prove that He was Divine to anyone by argument. When a man yields to Christ, perhaps without intelligent apprehension of all the truth concerning Him, and the Spirit takes possession of that man, then he *knows*. Did His disciples cease to be comrades? No, but they became men who, for the future, were not merely standing by Him, but were sharing one life with Him. Did they cease to be servants? No, they called themselves servants, and they gloried in it. Paul spoke of himself as "the bond-slave of Jesus Christ." [17] But their service now was the service of Christ in them, and that is what real Christian service is. In real Christian service you are not doing something to help Jesus Christ. You are at His absolute disposal, and He is doing things through you. That is the great secret. The Church, born that day, is the mystic Body of Christ Himself.

What difference did Pentecost make to the world at large? Before Pentecost there had been light. God has never left any people wholly without light. "In Him was life; and the life was the light of men." [18] That means that in Him was *all* life; all the life of all the creation in all its forms is centered on the Logos, the Christ. But, says John, in man life is light, in man there is not merely life, but an element of light also. "And the light shineth in the darkness; and the darkness apprehended it not." [19] The darkness did not extinguish it. It never did. "There was the true light, even the light that lighteth every man, coming into the world," [20] focused in a Person. The Spirit was poured out in two different applications. He was poured out upon the disciples, and He was also poured out upon all flesh. There came a new ministry into the world, a ministry of the Spirit interpreting Christ to the world. "He, when He is come, will convict the world in the matter of sin, in the matter of righteousness, and in the matter of judgment. Of sin, because they believe not on Me; of righteousness, because I go unto the Father, and ye behold Me no more; of judgment, because the prince of this world hath been judged." [21] But this ministry of conviction to the world depends upon the ministry of the Body of Christ, the Church. The Church was born to be the instrument of the Spirit. When the Church goes out to give her witness, the Spirit accompanies her, whether it be the witness of the apostle, or the witness of the prophet, or the evangelist, or the pastor and teacher, or the witness of Christian conversation. The world received a new ministry of conviction and a new ministry of constraint.

Has not this world of ours, wherever the church has gone and fulfilled her mission, felt the new constraint of the Spirit —the love of God, the light of God, and the life of God appearing to the world? That is the whole story of missionary work and of the missionary enterprise.

The new age that began at Pentecost is also characterized by limitations as to the Christ, as to the Church, and as to the world. In every case the resources are limitless; the resources of Christ wherein and whereby He can fulfill the Divine intention and purpose. Limitless and plenteous. I do not want to get into a theological controversy here, but I cannot hold with any man who talks about redemption only for a certain number. "God so loved the *world*. . . ." [22] I am not saying that God's grace is going to be *appropriated* by everyone. That is another matter; but there are resources in Christ that can meet all the world's need—limitless resources. Then is He in any sense limited? Yes, He is limited in His Body, the Church, and so in His work, the limitation growing progressively less and less as that Church grows up into Him in all things, Who is the Head. It is a solemn consideration for the Church that she can limit our Lord's mission in the world. Does someone ask, What do you mean by that? I mean this: He cannot reach that soul out yonder that He fain would bless, unless He has your feet to travel on, your eyes to see through, your lips through which to speak, and your hands through which to minister. Frances Ridley Havergal knew that when she wrote the hymn:

> Take my life and let it be
> Consecrated, Lord, to Thee.

You remember the words: "Take my feet; take my hands; take my voice; take my silver and my gold. . . ." The Lord of life is limited in His Church. It is a wise limitation, I know, because He has so limited Himself. The outpouring of the Spirit waits the cooperation of the members of His Church.

What about the Church, then. She has limitless resources. She has everything she needs to do her work in the world. It is at her disposal in her Lord by the Spirit. Do you say, She needs money? Oh, no, she does not. She has all the money she needs if it is consecrated within her own borders. To dwell on the material for a moment—there is plenty of money within the Church today to do God's word without the Church having to demean herself and her Lord by going to the world to ask for it. The trouble is that the Lord seemingly cannot get hold of that which belongs to Him.

But when I spoke of resources I was thinking in the high, the ultimate realm. We have all the power we need, all the wisdom we need to do our work. We have it in Christ through the ministry of the Holy Spirit. The Church is only limited within herself when she grieves or quenches the Spirit. There are three words of warning: "Grieve not the Holy Spirit," [23] "Resist [not] the Holy Spirit," [24] "Quench not the Spirit." [25] The resistance is the attitude of the world to the Spirit; the man *outside* the Church can do that. For those inside the fellowship of the Church there are two things we may do. We may grieve the Spirit; that is personal. The Greek word is poignant, meaning to cause sorrow to the Spirit of God. And in proportion as I do that in my own personal life, I am limiting the Church's power and Christ's mission. We may quench the Spirit. That word has to do with service, with the fire, impulse, and energy. If I do that I am also limiting the Church and the Christ of God.

What about the world? Limitless resources are at her disposal, everything she needs to solve her problems. Christ is the only solution for the world's sorrow and the world's sins. Is the world limited at all? She is limited when the Church fails to function properly. She is also limited by her own capacity for resistance. At that point our responsibility ceases.

There has been no lessening of the Church's resources since that day. This is still the day of Pentecost. The Spirit of God and the Christ of God through the Holy Spirit were no more at the disposal of that first group of disciples than they are to us, here and now, in this very hour. Let us not go about saying that what we need is more of the Spirit. It is not so, beloved. Put it the true way. What the Spirit needs is more of us, completely at His disposal. Do not go about saying, We are waiting for the Spirit. What is this I hear about "tarrying meetings"? Nothing is so contradictory to the genius of the New Testament. Jesus told His disciples to tarry in Jerusalem until the Spirit came, but never after. When the Spirit came, He came to abide. There is no need to wait for the Spirit. Rather, the Spirit is waiting for the Church, waiting for the opening of the highways of our own personality. You and I can go out now, filled with the Spirit.

May I close with a story by way of illustration. Years ago, in the days of sailing ships, a ship with no steam power was away out at sea. She became becalmed for days, weeks and months, as sometimes did happen, waiting for a breath of wind. The supply of water was low, and presently it was gone. There was plenty of food, but no water; at last those sailors were literally dying of thirst. "Water, water, everywhere, but not a drop to drink." [26] Then one day, as they lay almost exhausted, some already dying, they saw a steamer on the horizon coming towards them. Gathering up all their remaining strength they ran a signal up the masthead: "Dying for water." They were shocked in desperation when the steamer, instead of coming on towards them, began changing its course, and they thought, What cruelty is this? But first the steamer sent a signal back: "Dip your buckets." At first they thought it a most devilish, cruel taunt, until one man said, "Let's try." They lowered a bucket into the water, and when they pulled it up, one, more eager than the rest, plunged in his hand, tasted, and cried, "It *is* fresh!" and it *was* fresh water! They had drifted into the current of the Amazon. That mighty river is of such quantity and bulk that it throws its waters four hundred miles out to sea before it mingles with the ocean. There they were, right in the midst of fresh water, yet dying of thirst! Do you see the meaning of the parable? Dip your buckets! Don't sigh and blame God if you are devoid of the power of the Holy Spirit. It is all about you.

We are living in the age of Pentecost. God help us to open up all the avenues of our lives, and let Him flow in. Then we shall indeed be members of the Body of Christ, through Whom He can reveal God to men, and administer His great redemption.

Notes

CHAPTER 1

1. I Timothy 3:15,16.
2. I Corinthians 12:3.
3. Exodus 12:2.
4. I Corinthians 5:7,8.
5. I Corinthians 5:8.
6. I Corinthians 15:20
7. Luke 9:31.
8. Revelations 21:3.
9. Acts 1:6.
10. John 7:6.
11. See Foreword note re locale, also Dr. Morgan's volume on Acts, p. 24.
12. Luke 13:35.

CHAPTER 2

1. I Corinthians 14:19.
2. John 14:16.
3. Luke 22:31.
4. Luke 24:18 (free translation).
5. I Peter 1:3.
6. Luke 12:49,50.
7. Philippians 2:6,7.
8. Colossians 1:19.
9. Hebrews 1:3.
10. Luke 4:18.
11. I Corinthians 6:17.
12. John 16:7.

13. I John 1:1.
14. Philippians 2:5,6.
15. Luke 9:23.
16. I Peter 2:9.
17. Colossians 1:24.
18. John 7:37,38.
19. Romans 8:9.
20. John 3:8.
21. John 4:14.
22. John 7:38,39.
23. Matthew 3:11.
24. Ezekiel 47:9.

CHAPTER 3

1. 1 Corinthians 12:11.
2. Isaiah 61:3.
3. Ephesians 5:18.
4. Acts 26:14.

CHAPTER 4

1. Matthew 23:8.
2. Acts 2:4,14; 26:25.
3. Acts 26:24,25.
4. I Corinthians 2:2.
5. Romans 8:34.
6. Matthew 16:17-20.
7. John 20:28.
8. Psalms 16:8-11.
9. Proverbs 11:30.
10. Acts 17:22.

CHAPTER 5

1. Ephesians 5:18.
2. Acts 2:18.
3. Joel 2:30,31.
4. Joel 2:32.
5. Joel 2:32.

6. Joel 3:1,2.
7. John 16:7-11.
8. John 1:1,14.
9. Numbers 11:29.
10. Ephesians 5:18 (KJV).

CHAPTER 6

1. John 1:45,46.
2. Mark 1:24.
3. Matthew 21:11.
4. John 18:7.
5. Mark 14:67.
6. John 19:19.
7. Mark 16:6.
8. Luke 24:19.
9. Zechariah 3:1.
10. Numbers 13:16 (KJV).
11. Matthew 1:21.
12. I Corinthians 15:45,47.
13. John 1:26 (KJV).
14. Matthew 16:21.
15. Luke 22:28.
16. Mark 14:50 (KJV).
17. John 11:23,24.

CHAPTER 7

1. I Corinthians 15:5-8.
2. Philippians 2:5.
3. Philippians 2:6-7.
4. Hebrews 2:16.
5. Isaiah 14:12-14.
6. John 12:49.
7. John 8:28,29.
8. John 9:4.
9. John 4:34.
10. Acts 2:25.
11. Isaiah 14:14.
12. Acts 2:25.
13. Ezekiel 18:4.

14. John 10:18.
15. I Peter 2:24.

CHAPTER 8

1. John 21:25.
2. Psalms 110:1.
3. Matthew 6:26.
4. Genesis 1:26.
5. John 19:30.
6. Hebrews 9:14 (KJV).
7. Luke 24:49.
8. Acts 1:4.
9. John 7:37-39.
10. John 1:1,14.
11. Luke 7:32.
12. Philippians 2:6-11.
13. Revelation 5:6 (KJV).
14. John 15:26.
15. Matthew 22:32.
16. Matthew 21:23.
17. Matthew 22:17.
18. Matthew 22:28.
19. Matthew 22:36.
20. Matthew 22:41-42.
21. Matthew 22:44.

CHAPTER 9

1. I Peter 4:17 (KJV).
2. Acts 5:32.
3. Acts 16:30.
4. Acts 16:31.
5. Proverbs 23:7.
6. Isaiah 55:7.
7. Matthew 28:19.
8. Luke 2:40.
9. Luke 2:52.
10. Acts 2:42.
11. Malachi 3:16.
12. Malachi 3:17.

13. G. Rawson.
14. Psalms 50:23.

CHAPTER 10

1. Isaiah 61:1-2.
2. Luke 4:18-19.
3. John 16:28.
4. Luke 9:31.
5. II Corinthians 2:11.
6. John 1:5.
7. John 1:9.
8. John 1:18.
9. John 1:18.
10. Luke 12:49-50.
11. I Peter 2:9.
12. Luke 22:11.
13. Luke 22:27-28.
14. Luke 22:35.
15. John 15:15 (KJV).
16. I Corinthians 2:16.
17. Romans 1:1.
18. John 1:4.
19. John 1:5.
20. John 1:9.
21. John 16:8-11.
22. John 3:16.
23. Ephesians 4:30.
24. Acts 7:51.
25. I Thessalonians 5:19.
26. Samuel Taylor Coleridge.